NOTHING IS TOO TRIVIAL...

Finding your way through this cunning maze of
questions won't be easy, but with quick wits and
a memory for minutiae, you too can be a
quizmaster. So sharpen your trivial knowledge
and get an edge on your friends with

IN SEARCH OF
TRIVIA

JEFF ROVIN, a Trivial Pursuit™ fanatic, is the editor
of *Videogaming Illustrated* magazine and is about to
release a new magazine called *Trivia!* He is also the
author of many books, including *Winning at Trivial
Pursuit*™, *The Signet Books of TV Lists* and the soon-
to-be-published *TV Babylon*.

IN SEARCH OF
TRIVIA

by
Jeff Rovin
Editor of *Trivial* Magazine

A SIGNET BOOK

SIGNET
Published by the Penguin Group
Penguin Books USA Inc., 375 Hudson Street,
New York, New York 10014, U.S.A.
Penguin Books Ltd, 27 Wrights Lane,
London W8 5TZ, England
Penguin Books Australia Ltd, Ringwood,
Victoria, Australia
Penguin Books Canada Ltd, 10 Alcorn Avenue,
Toronto, Ontario, Canada M4V 3B2
Penguin Books (N.Z.) Ltd, 182–190 Wairau Road,
Auckland 10, New Zealand

Penguin Books Ltd, Registered Offices:
Harmondsworth, Middlesex, England

Published by Signet, an imprint of New American Library,
a division of Penguin Books USA Inc.

First Printing, July, 1984
12

 REGISTERED TRADEMARK—MARCA REGISTRADA

Printed in the United States of America

Contents

Preface

Whether you are a seasoned trivialist or a curious novice, look no further than these pages for the most exciting trivial search of your life. Within the sections that follow are 2,400 all-new questions guaranteed to delight, perplex, and challenge you—regardless of your age or level of trivial experience.

The questions for *In Search of Trivia* are grouped in four master categories: Popular Culture, The Decades, People, and Leisure Activities. Within each of these master categories are six topics—questions that cover favorite subjects such as movies, sports, rock and roll, TV and science, while at the same time mining rich but overlooked veins of trivia such as magazines, advertising, the Bible, and famous couples.

What's more, so that you won't have to go skipping around the book for correct answers, *In Search of Trivia* has been designed so that the questions are on the right-hand page of the book, with the answers conveniently located on the following left-hand page.

Whether you use these questions to play trivia games, stump your friends or spouse, or give your own memory a workout, you will find that joining the trivia explosion can be exciting, entertaining, and enlightening. So open to the first group of questions and see if you don't agree that searching for trivia is the most fun a person can have without working up a sweat.

PART ONE

POPULAR CULTURE

Popular Culture 1

BOOKS
Name the brothers who founded the *Guinness Book of World Records*.

ADVERTISING
What toothpaste made you "wonder where the yellow went"?

ROCK
Of the four musicians in Van Halen, how many are brothers?

TV
What 1960s series followed the exploits of Kelly Robinson and Alexander Scott?

MOVIES
What was the only Cecil B. DeMille film ever to win Best Picture of the Year?

MAGAZINES
What subject is covered in the magazine *Bondage*?

Popular Culture 2

BOOKS
What is the subtitle of *Slaughterhouse Five*?

ADVERTISING
What are the four names in the company that John Houseman says *earns* their money?

ROCK
Name the film starring rock idol Prince.

TV
What was Detective Fish's name on *Barney Miller*?

MOVIES
How many children did Captain von Trapp have in *The Sound of Music*?

MAGAZINES
Nova was the working title of what successful magazine?

Answers: Popular Culture 1

BOOKS
Ross and Norris McWhirter

ADVERTISING
Pepsodent

ROCK
Two: Edward and Alex

TV
I Spy

MOVIES
The Greatest Show on Earth

MAGAZINES
James Bond

Answers: Popular Culture 2

BOOKS
The Children's Crusade

ADVERTISING
Smith, Barney, Harris, Upham

ROCK
Purple Rain

TV
Phil

MOVIES
Seven

MAGAZINES
Omni

4

Popular Culture 3

BOOKS
What is the name of Sid Caesar's autobiography?

ADVERTISING
Which company made the aging, hearing-impaired Clara Peller famous?

ROCK
Who was Tina Turner's singing husband?

TV
What was the name of Antonio Fargas's embraceable character on *Starsky & Hutch*?

MOVIES
What famous swinging character has been played by James H. Pierce, Mike Henry, and Lex Barker?

MAGAZINES
What caped character was introduced in *Detective Comics* #27?

Popular Culture 4

BOOKS
Structurally, Henry Wadsworth Longfellow's *Tales of a Wayside Inn* most closely resembles what fourteenth-century classic?

ADVERTISING
Which tall man sold "good things from the garden?"

ROCK
What song was parodied by Weird Al Yankovic's "Eat It"?

TV
What bizarre series featured characters named Puglsey, Wednesday, and Gomez?

MOVIES
In what film did Gene Kelly and Frank Sinatra romp atop the Empire State Building?

MAGAZINES
What magazine used to boast of a circulation of 7,777,777?

Answers: Popular Culture 3

BOOKS
Where Have I Been?

ADVERTISING
Wendy's: She's the woman who asked, "Where's the beef"?

ROCK
Ike Turner

TV
Huggy Bear

MOVIES
Tarzan

MAGAZINES
Batman

Answers: Popular Culture 4

BOOKS
The Canterbury Tales

ADVERTISING
The Green Giant

ROCK
"Beat It"

TV
The Addams Family

MOVIES
On the Town

MAGAZINES
Better Homes and Gardens

Popular Culture 5

BOOKS
Name the novel that inspired the TV series *The Six Million Dollar Man*.

ADVERTISING
Which cigarette brand ran print ads about "the taste of success"?

ROCK
What was the first number-one Beatles hit in America?

TV
Who was the only *Partridge Family* star with the same first name as his or her character?

MOVIES
The climax of what Steven Spielberg film takes place at Devil's Tower?

MAGAZINE
What was the original name of *TV Guide*?

Popular Culture 6

BOOKS
What doomed and fallen Poe hero had a sister named Madeline?

ADVERTISING
Which one of these has not been a Pepsi slogan?   (a) "The pause that refreshes"   (b) "Come alive!"   (c) "Taste that beats the others cold"

ROCK
What German band had a 1984 hit entitled "Love At First Sting"?

TV
What was the name of the bumbling sergeant on Walt Disney's *Zorro*?

MOVIES
What roles did Claude Rains and Vivien Leigh play in the 1945 adaptation of a George Bernard Shaw play?

MAGAZINES
What magazine was Michael Douglas reading in the smugglers' plane in the 1984 film *Romancing the Stone*?

Answers: Popular Culture 5

BOOKS
Cyborg

ADVERTISING
Vantage

ROCK
I Want to Hold Your Hand

TV
Danny Bonaduce

MOVIES
Close Encounters of the Third Kind

MAGAZINES
TV Digest

Answers: Popular Culture 6

BOOKS
Roderick Usher

ADVERTISING
"The pause that refreshes"

ROCK
The Scorpions

TV
Garcia

MOVIES
Caesar and Cleopatra

MAGAZINES
Rolling Stone

Popular Culture 7

BOOKS
Which one of these was not written by priest Andrew M. Greeley? (a) *Lord of the Dance* (b) *Ascent Into Hell* (c) *Seeds of Yesterday*

ADVERTISING
What musical superstar hit the big time after doing commercials for McDonald's and State Farm Insurance?

ROCK
Name the make of car mentioned in *Fun, Fun, Fun* by the Beach Boys.

TV
Name the young boy taken in by George and Katherine Papadopolis.

MOVIES
What comedy, originally planned for Bob Hope and Danny Kaye, is about two musicians who witness the St. Valentine's Day Massacre?

MAGAZINES
What magazine has a Reagan daughter-in-law on its editorial staff?

Popular Culture 8

BOOKS
Name the two sequels to Frederik Pohl's award-winning science fiction novel *Gateway*.

ADVERTISING
What unlikely product did Coty market in the sixties by declaring "Nobody who loves mini, kicky, bare-as-you-dare fashions looked dressed without it"?

ROCK
What Kenny Loggins smash hit came from a motion picture sound track?

TV
What game-show host is famous for kissing female contestants?

MOVIES
Give the English translation of the 1964 Sophia Loren Italian classic, *Ieri, Oggi e Domani*.

MAGAZINES
Whose nude photo spread in *Playboy*'s December, 1983, issue caused the magazine to sell out?

Answers: Popular Culture 7

BOOKS
c) *Seeds of Yesterday*

ADVERTISING
Barry Manilow

ROCK
A Thunderbird or T-bird

TV
Webster

MOVIES
Some Like It Hot

MAGAZINES
Interview

Answers: Popular Culture 8

BOOKS
Beyond the Blue Event Horizon and *Heechee Rendezvous*

ADVERTISING
Body paint

ROCK
Footloose

TV
Richard Dawson

MOVIES
Yesterday, Today, and Tomorrow

MAGAZINES
Joan Collins

Popular Culture 9

BOOKS
Who wrote *The Trial* and *Metamorphosis*?

ADVERTISING
What shampoo called itself "The beauty soap for your hair"?

ROCK
What was totally eclipsed in Bonnie Tyler's 1983 hit?

TV
What adjective preceded Phyllis Diller's name in the title of her fall 1968 series?

MOVIES
What did David Niven and Anthony Quinn help to blow up in 1961?

MAGAZINES
What is the magazine published by the American Museum of Natural History?

Popular Culture 10

BOOKS
True or false: The third-century dramatist Kalidasa is widely considered the "Shakespeare of India."

ADVERTISING
What acne lotion came on the market by advertising itself as "a man's medication"?

ROCK
By what name is Gordon Sumner popularly known to fans?

TV
Name the 1960s war series set in the North African desert.

MOVIES
What store did Natalie Wood work for in *Love with the Proper Stranger*?

MAGAZINES
What was the name of *TV Guide*'s ill-fated companion magazine about television?

BOOKS
Franz Kafka

ADVERTISING
Breck

ROCK
The heart

TV
Beautiful

MOVIES
The Guns of Navarone

MAGAZINES
Natural History

BOOKS
True

ADVERTISING
Tackle

ROCK
Sting

TV
The Rat Patrol

MOVIES
Macy's

MAGAZINES
Panorama

Popular Culture 11

BOOKS
Name the novel written about Vincent Van Gogh's life.

ADVERTISING
Apart from your health, you "know what counts" if you smoke this brand of cigarette.

ROCK
What synchronic three-man band sent a "Message in a Bottle"?

TV
Which three *M*A*S*H* soldiers were carried over in *AfterM*A*S*H*?

MOVIES
What two actresses sang "When Love Goes Wrong" in *Gentlemen Prefer Blondes*?

MAGAZINES
What magazine provides "A limited warranty to consumers: Replacement or refund if defective"?

Popular Culture 12

BOOKS
Which one of these is not an Alistair MacLean novel?   (a) *The Satan Bug*   (b) *Eight Million Ways to Die*   (c) *Floodgate*

ADVERTISING
What famous soft drink was originally called Patio Diet Cola?

ROCK
What backup group consisted of Joyce Vincent and Thelma Hopkins?

TV
What was McHale's rank in *McHale's Navy*?

MOVIES
What musical instrument did Jack Nicholson play in *Five Easy Pieces*?

MAGAZINES
What magazine features departments entitled "Picks & Pans" and "Chatter"?

Answers: Popular Culture 11

BOOKS
Lust For Life

ADVERTISING
Kent III

ROCK
The Police

TV
Colonel Potter, Father Mulcahy, and Klinger

MOVIES
Marilyn Monroe and Jane Russell

MAGAZINES
Good Housekeeping

Answers: Popular Culture 12

BOOKS
b) *Eight Million Ways to Die*

ADVERTISING
Diet Pepsi

ROCK
Dawn, of Tony Orlando and Dawn

TV
Lieutenant Commander

MOVIES
The piano

MAGAZINES
People

Popular Culture 13

BOOKS
What did Mencken's initials, H. L., stand for?

ADVERTISING
What were Max Factor's Pink-a-pades?

ROCK
What number precedes the "Ragged Tiger" in the Duran Duran album title?

TV
At what eatery does *Alice* work?

MOVIES
On what kind of vessel did Anthony Perkins serve in *On the Beach*?

MAGAZINES
What women's magazine was launched by *New York* in the 1970s?

Popular Culture 14

BOOKS
Before he courted and won the Countess Lyndon, what was Barry Lyndon's name?

ADVERTISING
What were the first three monster models manufactured by Aurora Products in the early sixties?

ROCK
Who was the first member of The Monkees to quit the band?

TV
What series was about Bentley Gregg and his niece Kelly?

MOVIES
What war was the setting of Elvis Presley's first film, *Love Me Tender*?

MAGAZINES
What did *The Ladies' Home Journal* celebrate in January, 1984?

Answers: Popular Culture 13

BOOKS
Henry Louis

ADVERTISING
Pink lipsticks and nail polishes

ROCK
Seven

TV
Mel's Café

MOVIES
A submarine

MAGAZINES
Ms.

Answers: Popular Culture 14

BOOKS
Redmond Barry

ADVERTISING
Frankenstein, Dracula, and the Wolfman

ROCK
Peter Tork

TV
Bachelor Father

MOVIES
The Civil War

MAGAZINES
Its one-hundredth birthday

Popular Culture 15

BOOKS
What publishing imprint is headed by Donald A. Wollheim, the doyen of science-fiction editors?

ADVERTISING
Of what words is "Sanka" a contraction?

ROCK
What group is composed of Gibbs?

TV
What was Lionel's last name on *All in the Family*?

MOVIES
What actor was spared a whipping when Moses broke his tormentor's back in *The Ten Commandments*?

MAGAZINES
What was the name of *Newsweek*'s short-lived sports magazine?

Popular Culture 16

BOOKS
True or false: *Moby-Dick*'s full title is *Moby-Dick: Or, The Whale*.

ADVERTISING
What animal has had a cigarette brand named after it?

ROCK
"Take a Look At Me Now" is the subtitle of what 1984 hit?

TV
Name the two series hosted by Rod Serling.

MOVIES
In what movie did Cliff Robertson play the part of a retarded man who became a genius?

MAGAZINES
Meg Greenfield and George F. Will are regular columnists for what magazine?

Answers: Popular Culture 15

BOOKS
DAW Books

ADVERTISING
Sans caffeine (sic)

ROCK
The Bee Gees

TV
Jefferson

MOVIES
John Derek

MAGAZINES
Inside Sports

Answers: Popular Culture 16

BOOKS
True

ADVERTISING
Camel

ROCK
"Against All Odds"

TV
The Twilight Zone and *Night Gallery*

MOVIES
Charly

MAGAZINES
Newsweek

Popular Culture 17

BOOKS
Who wrote *The Butter Battle Book*? (a) Julia Child (b) Weight Watchers (c) Dr. Seuss

ADVERTISING
True or False: Ronald Reagan once appeared on the cover of a box of Kellogg's Corn Flakes.

ROCK
What wholesome singer/star is the most famous alumnus of the Chad Mitchell Trio?

TV
Who portrayed The Dollmaker in the TV movie of the same name?

MOVIES
Name the sequel to *Gentlemen Prefer Blondes*.

MAGAZINES
In the movie *The Big Chill*, which magazine did the character Michael work for?

Popular Culture 18

BOOKS
What dashing movie star wrote the splendid adventure novels *Beam Ends* and *Showdown*?

ADVERTISING
What publication boasts, "All the business news you need. When you need it."

ROCK
What's "a battlefield" according to singer Pat Benatar?

TV
Which famous Western opened each week with the burning of a map?

MOVIES
What was the name of Marlon Brando's character in *A Streetcar Named Desire*?

MAGAZINES
Is it *Ms.*, *Cosmopolitan*, or *The Ladies' Home Journal* which warns, "Never Underestimate the Power of a Woman"?

Answers: Popular Culture 17

BOOKS
c) Dr. Seuss

ADVERTISING
False

ROCK
John Denver

TV
Jane Fonda

MOVIES
Gentlemen Marry Brunettes

MAGAZINES
People

Answers: Popular Culture 18

BOOKS
Errol Flynn

ADVERTISING
The Wall Street Journal

ROCK
Love

TV
Bonanza

MOVIES
Stanley Kowalski

MAGAZINES
The Ladies' Home Journal

Popular Culture 19

BOOKS
Who was Anne Hathaway's celebrated author-husband?

ADVERTISING
Who manufactures the Civic?

ROCK
What famous song features these lyrics: "Sont des mots qui vont très bien ensemble"?

TV
What Florida-based sitcom couple was wed on December 2, 1969?

MOVIES
The Young Lions was the first English-language film of what future Oscar-winning actor?

MAGAZINES
What publication is subtitled "Fitness of Body and Mind"?

Popular Culture 20

BOOKS
True or false: Mark Twain and Western writer Bret Harte collaborated on the play *Ah Sin*.

ADVERTISING
What whiskey's initials, CC, appear in gold on the label?

ROCK
What singer's sisters are named Rebbie, Janet, and LaToya?

TV
On what game show did contestants receive "zonks"?

MOVIES
What crime had Elvis Presley allegedly committed in *Jailhouse Rock*?

MAGAZINES
What superhero made his debut in *Amazing Fantasy* #15, using the title's first word as part of his name?

Answers: Popular Culture 19

BOOKS
William Shakespeare

ADVERTISING
Honda

ROCK
"Michelle," by John Lennon and Paul McCartney

TV
Captain Tony Nelson and Jeannie of *I Dream of Jeannie*

MOVIES
Maximillian Schell

MAGAZINES
American Health

Answers: Popular Culture 20

BOOKS
True

ADVERTISING
Canadian Club

ROCK
Michael Jackson

TV
Let's Make a Deal

MOVIES
Murder

MAGAZINES
The Amazing Spider-Man

Popular Culture 21

BOOKS
What black character's adventures, later the subject of a Walt Disney film, were chronicled by writer Joel Chandler Harris?

ADVERTISING
"One out of every three trucks on the road is _____"

ROCK
Who was the lead singer of Blue Angel?

TV
What series was set in the General Pershing Veterans Administration Hospital?

MOVIES
What American star played the lecherous Komarovsky in *Doctor Zhivago*?

MAGAZINES
For which of the following magazines did George Harrison's first wife, Patti Boyd Harrison, once write a column? (a) *Teen* (b) *Sixteen* (c) *Seventeen*

Popular Culture 22

BOOKS
What is the name of Truman Capote's long-awaited roman à clef about his famous friends?

ADVERTISING
What car was advertised early in 1984 with the slogan, "A legend turns 20"?

ROCK
What was Mason Williams's first and biggest hit?

TV
What 1950s Western co-starred X. Brands as Pahoo-Ka-Ta-Wah?

MOVIES
In what 1982 film did Malcolm McDowell turn into a panther?

MAGAZINES
True or false: *Mad* Magazine once released a record that consisted entirely of music and burps.

Answers: Popular Culture 21

BOOKS
Uncle Remus

ADVERTISING
Ford

ROCK
Cyndi Lauper

TV
AfterM*A*S*H

MOVIES
Rod Steiger

MAGAZINES
b) *Sixteen*

Answers: Popular Culture 22

BOOKS
Answered Prayers

ADVERTISING
Mustang

ROCK
"Classical Gas"

TV
Yancy Derringer

MOVIES
The Cat People

MAGAZINES
True

Popular Culture 23

BOOKS
What novel was instrumental in getting President Roosevelt behind the Pure Food and Drug Act?

ADVERTISING
What was Elsa Miranda's nom-de-fruit?

ROCK
What group had hits in the late 1960s with "Yummy, Yummy, Yummy" and "Chewy, Chewy"?

TV
When Redd Foxx and Demond Wilson left *Sanford and Son*, what did the series' title become?

MOVIES
In which one of her movies does Barbra Streisand sing to flowers?

MAGAZINES
What has the largest circulation of any Sunday magazine supplement?

Popular Culture 24

BOOKS
What is the best-selling novel of all time?

ADVERTISING
In rental ads, what does the phrase "riv vu" mean?

ROCK
What group was formed in 1971 by Fred Mercury, Brian May, John Deacon, and Roger Meadows Taylor?

TV
What was the name of Jerry Helper's wife on *The Dick Van Dyke Show*?

MOVIES
Name the Elizabeth Taylor/Montgomery Clift film made from Theodore Dreiser's *An American Tragedy*.

MAGAZINES
What magazine presents the annual Dubious Achievement Awards?

Answers: Popular Culture 23

BOOKS
The Jungle (by Upton Sinclair)

ADVERTISING
Chiquita Banana

ROCK
The Ohio Express

TV
The Sanford Arms

MOVIES
On a Clear Day You Can See Forever

MAGAZINES
Parade

Answers: Popular Culture 24

BOOKS
Valley of the Dolls

ADVERTISING
River view

ROCK
Queen

TV
Millie

MOVIES
A Place in the Sun

MAGAZINES
Esquire

Popular Culture 25

BOOKS
What book is subtitled "Lessons from America's Best-run Companies"?

ADVERTISING
What was Johnny Roventini's immortal call?

ROCK
Who had hits in 1984 with "The Heart of Rock 'n' Roll" and "I Want a New Drug"?

TV
In what city did the Bob Newhart character, psychologist Robert Hartley, practice?

MOVIES
In what science-fiction film did Rod Taylor fall in love with an Eloi named Weena?

MAGAZINES
What is the name of the magazine published by the American Film Institute?

Popular Culture 26

BOOKS
What was Shakespeare's last play?

ADVERTISING
What does FTD stand for?

ROCK
The album *Buddah & the Chocolate Box* was the work of what band?

TV
What was the name of the short-lived 1976 baseball series based on a book by Jim Bouton?

MOVIES
What Roman emperor did Peter Ustinov play in *Quo Vadis*?

MAGAZINES
Which children's magazine features the adventures of Goofus and Gallant?

BOOKS
In Search of Excellence

ADVERTISING
"Call for Phillip Morris!"

ROCK
Huey Lewis and the News

TV
Chicago

MOVIES
The Time Machine

MAGAZINES
American Film

Answers: Popular Culture 26

BOOKS
The Tempest

ADVERTISING
Florists Transworld Delivery

ROCK
Cat Stevens

TV
Ball Four

MOVIES
Nero

MAGAZINES
Highlights for Children

Popular Culture 27

BOOKS
What is the full title of Robert Louis Stevenson's story about Dr. Jekyll and Mr. Hyde?

ADVERTISING
True or false: The original Log Cabin syrup container was a tin log cabin.

ROCK
What is Ozzie Osbourne's real name?

TV
What is Fonzie's full name?

MOVIES
How many men went canoeing in *Deliverance*?

MAGAZINES
What is the organization behind *Boy's Life*?

Popular Culture 28

BOOKS
What is the name of the novel *The Wolf of the Steppes* in its native tongue?

ADVERTISING
What was Dr. Bunting's Remedy called after eczema was found to be among the conditions it healed?

ROCK
In what city did Jimi Hendrix die?

TV
What city was the setting for *One Day At a Time*?

MOVIES
Who wrote *The Heartbreak Kid*?

MAGAZINES
What is the leading publication for the advertising industry?

Answers: Popular Culture 27

BOOKS
The Strange Case of Dr. Jekyll and Mr. Hyde

ADVERTISING
True

ROCK
John Osbourne

TV
Arthur Fonzarelli

MOVIES
Four

MAGAZINES
The Boy Scouts of America

Answers: Popular Culture 28

BOOKS
Steppenwolf (aka *Der Steppenwolf*)

ADVERTISING
Noxzema ("knocks eczema")

ROCK
London

TV
Indianapolis

MOVIES
Neil Simon

MAGAZINES
Advertising Age

Popular Culture 29

BOOKS
How did poet Percy Bysshe Shelley meet his death?

ADVERTISING
Not to get syrupy, but who was Nancy Green, a famous black cook from Kentucky?

ROCK
According to singer Randy Newman, which human beings "don't deserve to live"?

TV
What popular series was about Tom and Eddie Corbett?

MOVIES
Who played the girl who could cook without a stove in *Firestarter*?

MAGAZINES
Which magazine caused great controversy when it suggested that Teddy Kennedy would be President if he had driven a Volkswagen in Chappaquiddick?

Popular Culture 30

BOOKS
Which one of these Stephen King books is nonfiction? (a) *Night Shift* (b) *Danse Macabre* (c) *The Shining*

ADVERTISING
What kind of bird is used to advertise Fruit Loops?

ROCK
What group had a big hit in 1965 with "This Diamond Ring"?

TV
What was the name of the character that replaced Emma Peel on *The Avengers*?

MOVIES
Name the future husband and wife team that starred in *Caveman* in 1981.

MAGAZINES
What is the name of the children's version of *Ebony*?

BOOKS
He drowned

ADVERTISING
The real Aunt Jemima

ROCK
Short People

TV
The Courtship of Eddie's Father

MOVIES
Drew Barrymore

MAGAZINES
National Lampoon

Answers: Popular Culture 30

BOOKS
b) *Danse Macabre*

ADVERTISING
A toucan

ROCK
Gary Lewis and the Playboys

TV
Tara King

MOVIES
Ringo Starr and Barbara Bach

MAGAZINES
Ebony Jr.

Popular Culture 31

BOOKS
True or false: Author Timothy Dexter, disgusted by the criticism over the lack of punctuation in his *A Pickle for the Knowing Ones*, published a page of nothing but punctuation marks in the book's second edition.

ADVERTISING
What product took its name from the number of compound-filled vases used in its development?

ROCK
Name the actor who had a huge hit in 1976 with *I'm Easy*.

TV
Before winning his Oscar, what black actor starred in *The Young Rebels* in 1970?

MOVIES
What was Paul Newman's profession in *The Young Philadelphians*?

MAGAZINES
What publication is famous for its "500"?

Popular Culture 32

BOOKS
What English author began his career by covering governmental affairs for *The Morning Chronicle*?

ADVERTISING
What TV-commercial character sailed a boat in a toilet?

ROCK
What member of the Mothers of Invention recorded "Don't Eat the Yellow Snow" in 1974?

TV
True or false: Danny Thomas played a water-breathing, thumbless alien in *The Dick Van Dyke Show*.

MOVIES
What 1975 film is subtitled, "...By an Unusual Destiny in the Blue Sea of August"?

MAGAZINES
What is the name of Hugh Hefner's puzzle magazine?

BOOKS
True

ADVERTISING
Vaseline

ROCK
Keith Carradine

TV
Lou Gossett, Jr.

MOVIES
A lawyer

MAGAZINES
Fortune

Answers: Popular Culture 32

BOOKS
Charles Dickens

ADVERTISING
The Tidy-Bowl Man

ROCK
Frank Zappa

TV
True

MOVIES
Swept Away

MAGAZINES
Games

Popular Culture 33

BOOKS
True or false: In *The Sun Also Rises*, Jake Barnes and Lady Brett Ashley became lovers.

ADVERTISING
What is New York's advertising slogan?

ROCK
What year did Zager and Evans sing about in 1969?

TV
Who was the middle child on *Bonanza*?

MOVIES
What film spawned the popular phrase, "Make my day"?

MAGAZINES
What magazine did Time, Inc., launch and kill in 1983 at a loss of over $47 million?

Popular Culture 34

BOOKS
True or false: Merriam-Webster created America's first dictionary.

ADVERTISING
In 1963, the National Oil Fuel Institute took out a series of ads in which they proclaimed all but one of the following. Which one did they *not* proclaim? (a) "You can slice up to $2,000 off the price of your new house with oil heat." (b) "In twenty years, oil heat will save many homeowners $6,000 a year." (c) "Oil heat is better for your skin than electric heat."

ROCK
Who was the most famous name to emerge from the group Faces?

TV
What was the name of Sergeant Preston's horse?

MOVIES
What country was the setting for *Twelve O'Clock High*?

MAGAZINES
Who is the editor-in-chief of *The National Review*?

BOOKS
False: A war accident made it impossible for Jake to be any woman's lover.

ADVERTISING
I Love New York.

ROCK
2525

TV
Hoss

MOVIES
Sudden Impact

MAGAZINES
TV-Cable Week

Answers: Popular Culture 34

BOOKS
False. Noah Webster created the dictionary. ("Merriam" was George and Charles Merriam, who bought the rights to Webster's dictionary)

ADVERTISING
c) "Oil heat is better for your skin than electric heat."

ROCK
Rod Stewart

TV
Rex

MOVIES
England

MAGAZINES
William F. Buckley

Popular Culture 35

BOOKS
Whose illustrations for Lewis Carroll's *Alice's Adventures in Wonderland* have become inseparable from the text?

ADVERTISING
What cigarette brand separated the men from the boys?

ROCK
What group counted superstars Stevie Nicks and Christine McVie among its members?

TV
Who hosted the highest-rated *Saturday Night Live* in the show's history?

MOVIES
What actor played the monster in Mel Brooks's *Young Frankenstein*?

MAGAZINES
What is the name of the magazine edited by George Plimpton?

Popular Culture 36

BOOKS
True or false: Alfred, Lord Tennyson, was more accurately the First Baron Tennyson.

ADVERTISING
True or false: Mallory Corporation once did a Christmas push coaxing the elderly to give their loved ones "the gift of sound" by purchasing Mallory Batteries for hearing aids.

ROCK
What is the stage name of Janis Fink?

TV
On the original *Three's Company*, who shared an apartment with Jack Tripper and Chrissy Snow?

MOVIES
What instrument did Leslie Howard play in *Intermezzo*?

MAGAZINES
Who is the mascot of the National Wildlife Federation's *Nature Magazine*?

Answers: Popular Culture 35

BOOKS
Sir John Tenniel

ADVERTISING
Lucky Strike

ROCK
Fleetwood Mac

TV
Mrs. Miskel Spillman (winner of the "anyone can host" contest)

MOVIES
Peter Boyle

MAGAZINES
The Paris Review

Answers: Popular Culture 36

BOOKS
True

ADVERTISING
True

ROCK
Janis Ian

TV
Janet Wood

MOVIES
Violin

MAGAZINES
Ranger Rick, a raccoon

Popular Culture 37

BOOKS
What character did the wolf impersonate in *Little Red Riding Hood?*

ADVERTISING
What product's ad campaign bemoaned, "I can't believe I ate the whole thing"?

ROCK
What is Paul McCartney's middle name?

TV
Who was Wild Bill Hickok's sidekick?

MOVIES
What 1981 movie marked James Cagney's return to the screen after twenty years?

MAGAZINES
Which magazine features the sarcastic comic strip "Mrs. Gipper"?   (a) *National Lampoon*   (b) *Punch*   (c) *Rolling Stone*

Popular Culture 38

BOOKS
What are the three *L*'s in Leo Buscaglia's best-selling title?

ADVERTISING
What movie megaflop was advertised, "What one loves about life are the things that fade"?

ROCK
What fictitious animal did the Irish Rovers sing about in 1968?

TV
Who was the son of Henry and Alice Mitchell?

MOVIES
What film featured John Travolta, Debra Winger, and a mechanical bull?

MAGAZINES
H. G. Brown is the editor of what trend-setting magazine?

BOOKS
The grandmother

ADVERTISING
Alka Seltzer

ROCK
Paul. His first name is James.

TV
Jingles

MOVIES
Ragtime

MAGAZINES
c) *Rolling Stone*

BOOKS
Living, Loving and Learning

ADVERTISING
Heaven's Gate

ROCK
The Unicorn

TV
Dennis (the Menace)

MOVIES
Urban Cowboy

MAGAZINES
Cosmopolitan

Popular Culture 39

BOOKS
What novel did Charles Dickens leave incomplete at the time of his death?

ADVERTISING
What car did John DeLorean announce as being "the Pontiac of the personal sports car field"?

ROCK
True or false: A 1959 Rock-A-Teens hit consisted entirely of the words "Woo hoo"?

TV
Which *Star Trek* character didn't beam aboard until the show's second season?

MOVIES
Raymond Massey did *not* play Abraham Lincoln in which of the following films? (a) *How the West Was Won* (b) *Young Mr. Lincoln* (c) *Abe Lincoln in Illinois*

MAGAZINES
For what newspaper did journalists Woodward and Bernstein write?

Popular Culture 40

BOOKS
Little girls are made of sugar, spice, and everything nice. What are little boys made of?

ADVERTISING
According to the commercial, where could you "meet the nicest people"?

ROCK
What group is composed of Agnetha, Bjorn, Benny, and Annifrid?

TV
On *Leave it to Beaver*, what was Lumpy's last name?

MOVIES
What animals undertook Walt Disney's *Incredible Journey*?

MAGAZINES
Which one of these magazines is not the basis of a popular trivia game? (a) *Newsweek* (b) *Time* (c) *People*

Answers: Popular Culture 39

BOOKS
The Mystery of Edwin Drood

ADVERTISING
The Firebird

ROCK
True

TV
Ensign Chekov

MOVIES
b) *Young Mr. Lincoln*

MAGAZINES
The Washington Post

Answers: Popular Culture 40

BOOKS
Frogs, snails, and puppy-dogs' tails

ADVERTISING
"On a Honda"

ROCK
ABBA

TV
Rutherford

MOVIES
Two dogs and a cat

MAGAZINES
a) *Newsweek*

Popular Culture 41

BOOKS
True or false: Jules Vernes's real name was Jean-Louis Jules Verne.

ADVERTISING
The grocery store initials A & P stand for: (a) Apples and Peaches (b) the Great Atlantic & Pacific Tea Company (c) Ale & Produce

ROCK
What group had hits in 1983–84 entitled "Gold," "True," and "Communication"?

TV
What was the name of Perry Mason's secretary?

MOVIES
Name the Scottish village visited by Gene Kelly and Van Johnson in the 1954 musical.

MAGAZINES
What magazine chronicled the adventures of the Man of Bronze and the Fabulous Five?

Popular Culture 42

BOOKS
To whom does the devil promise twenty-four years of happiness in Marlowe's classic play?

ADVERTISING
The Maxwell House of that coffee's brand name refers to: (a) the home of multimillionaire A. D. Maxwell (b) A freighter firm that imported coffee beans (c) a hotel

ROCK
Who recorded "Ne Ne Na Na Na Na Nu Nu" in 1958?

TV
Name the two Findlays of Bea Arthur's sitcom.

MOVIES
What real-life character was the subject of the 1942 film *Tennessee Johnson*?

MAGAZINES
The letters page of what magazine has a picture of a bomb in a mailbox?

Answers: Popular Culture 41

BOOKS
False

ADVERTISING
b) the Great Atlantic & Pacific Tea Company

ROCK
Spandau Ballet

TV
Della Street

MOVIES
Brigadoon

MAGAZINES
Doc Savage

Answers: Popular Culture 42

BOOKS
Dr. Faustus

ADVERTISING
c) a hotel

ROCK
Dickey Do and the Don'ts

TV
Maude and Walter

MOVIES
President Andrew Johnson

MAGAZINES
Mad

Popular Culture 43

BOOKS
What animal is described as "frumious" in Lewis Carroll's "Jabberwocky"?

ADVERTISING
George Plimpton was the spokesperson for what videogame system?

ROCK
Who was lead singer of the sixties group the Dreamers?

TV
What Western series was set at Fort Courage?

MOVIES
Who played Fletcher Christian in the 1933 film version of the Bounty saga, *In the Wake of the Bounty*?

MAGAZINES
In the early 1970s, the publisher of the hugely successful *Golf Digest* and *Tennis* flopped with a magazine about what sport?

Popular Culture 44

BOOKS
What famous American detective made his first appearance in 1886 in *The Old Detective's Pupil*?

ADVERTISING
At the turn of the century, Grain-O, a cereal beverage, was manufactured by a firm that made what other still-popular product?

ROCK
The Four Lovers became what better-known group?

TV
What were the respective vocations of Phoebe Figalilly and Harold Everett?

MOVIES
What historical character did Toshiro Mifune play four different times, most recently in *Midway*?

MAGAZINES
What organization publishes *Consumer Reports*?

Answers: Popular Culture 43

BOOKS
The Bandersnatch

ADVERTISING
Intellivision

ROCK
Freddie (Garrity)

TV
F Troop

MOVIES
Errol Flynn

MAGAZINES
Skiing

Answers: Popular Culture 44

BOOKS
Nick Carter

ADVERTISING
Jello-O

ROCK
The Four Seasons

TV
Nanny and the professor, of the series of the same name.

MOVIES
Admiral Yamamoto

MAGAZINES
Consumers Union

Popular Culture 45

BOOKS
Which of these was not written by H. G. Wells? (a) *The Sea Lady* (b) *Food of the Gods* (c) *Mysterious Island*

ADVERTISING
For what company did football player O. J. Simpson make his commercial debut?

ROCK
What rock group composed and performed the music for the film version of Stephen King's *Firestarter*?

TV
Bobby Rosengarden conducted the orchestra for what TV host?

MOVIES
What Robert E. Howard character was played on film by Arnold Schwarzenegger?

MAGAZINES
What biweekly publication is the only *People* knockoff to have survived?

Popular Culture 46

BOOKS
Who takes Darnay's place on the guillotine in Charles Dickens's *A Tale of Two Cities*?

ADVERTISING
What luggage company manufactures "the Survivor"?

ROCK
What was the 1970 chart-topper by Ernie of *Sesame Street*?

TV
What was Rhoda's last name in *The Mary Tyler Moore Show*?

MOVIES
What cult movie classic was advertised: "10 Seconds: The pain begins. 15 Seconds: You can't breathe. 20 Seconds: Your head explodes"?

MAGAZINES
What magazine was the stomping ground for Wicked Wanda?

BOOKS
c) *Mysterious Island*

ADVERTISING
Hertz Rent-a-Car

ROCK
Tangerine Dream

TV
Dick Cavett

MOVIES
Conan the Barbarian

MAGAZINES
Us

Answers: Popular Culture 46

BOOKS
Sydney Carton

ADVERTISING
Samsonite

ROCK
Rubber Duckie

TV
Morgenstern

MOVIES
Scanners

MAGAZINES
Penthouse

Popular Culture 47

BOOKS
Which is the correct spelling of Stephen King's novel? (a) *Pet Sematary* (b) *Pet Semetery* (c) *Pet Semetary*

ADVERTISING
How much was Alan Alda reportedly paid to appear in commercials for Atari computers? (a) $10 million (b) $5 million (c) $2.5 million

ROCK
What group had hits in the sixties with "Groovin'" and "A Beautiful Morning"?

TV
The 1977–78 anthology series was called *What Really Happened to the Class of:* (a) '55 (b) '65 (c) '75

MOVIES
The 1954 film, *The Sign of the Pagan*, was about the fall of what notoriously ruthless fifth-century figure?

MAGAZINES
What magazine did Diana Vreeland serve as editor-in-chief?

Popular Culture 48

BOOKS
True or false: Former policeman Joseph Wambaugh is the author of the 1984 best-seller *One Police Plaza*?

ADVERTISING
What are you advised not to leave home without?

ROCK
In 1959, where did Paul Anka suggest that you "Put Your Head"?

TV
Who was the host of *Hootenanny*?

MOVIES
What actor played Henry to Katharine Hepburn's Eleanor of Aquitaine?

MAGAZINES
What is the French magazine *Métal Hurlant* known as in the US?

BOOKS
a) *Pet Sematary*

ADVERTISING
a) $10 million

ROCK
The Rascals (aka the Young Rascals)

TV
b) '65

MOVIES
Attila the Hun

MAGAZINES
Vogue

Answers: Popular Culture 48

BOOKS
False. William H. Caunitz wrote it.

ADVERTISING
Your American Express card

ROCK
"On My Shoulder"

TV
Jack Linkletter

MOVIES
Peter O'Toole

MAGAZINES
Heavy Metal

Popular Culture 49

BOOKS
Was Evelyn Waugh a man or a woman?

ADVERTISING
Because of FDA regulations, what soap was forced to change its claim of 100% purity to 99 44/100%?

ROCK
Who was the first American artist to get label credit on a Beatles record?

TV
Name the character created on a computer by Desi Arnaz, Jr.

MOVIES
Agatha Christie's *And Then There Were None* was remade under what title in 1965 and 1975?

MAGAZINES
What is the full title of *The New York Review*?

Popular Culture 50

BOOKS
What is the blanket name for Don Pendleton's top-selling paper-back adventure series?

ADVERTISING
What name did C. W. Post give his breakfast cereal, Elijah's Manna, after the religious community came down on the name?

ROCK
Whom did Deniece Williams ask, "Let's Hear it For"?

TV
On *Fibber McGee and Molly*, what was Molly's last name?

MOVIES
In what hospital was the Doctor Kildare series set?

MAGAZINES
To what brand of computer is *Ahoy!* devoted?

BOOKS
A man

ADVERTISING
Ivory

ROCK
Billy Preston

TV
Automan

MOVIES
Ten Little Indians

MAGAZINES
The New York Review of Books

Answers: Popular Culture 50

BOOKS
The Executioner

ADVERTISING
Post Toasties

ROCK
"The Boy"

TV
McGee

MOVIES
Blair General

MAGAZINES
The Commodore 64

Popular Culture 51

BOOKS
What were the first names of the Brothers Grimm?

ADVERTISING
What company paid millions to The Jackson brothers for commercial representation?

ROCK
True or false: Jethro Tull is the lead singer of that group.

TV
Who hosted 1972's *"Wow" Show*?

MOVIES
Who is *Star Wars*'s most famous Wookiee?

MAGAZINES
What newspaper once put out a Sunday edition which weighed over seven pounds?

Popular Culture 52

BOOKS
In her book, what does Erma Bombeck call the Second Oldest Profession?

ADVERTISING
What is distinctive about Mr. Clean's head?

ROCK
What military figure was the subject of a 1960 Larry Verne hit?

TV
What was the first name of Private Eye Mannix?

MOVIES
What 1961 film was about Spain's national hero, Rodrigo Diaz de Bivar?

MAGAZINES
What magazine's editorial page is called "As We See It"?

Answers: Popular Culture 51

BOOKS
Jacob and Wilhelm

ADVERTISING
Pepsi

ROCK
False. He was an eighteenth-century agriculturist

TV
Ken Berry

MOVIES
Chewbacca

MAGAZINES
The New York Times

Answers: Popular Culture 52

BOOKS
Motherhood

ADVERTISING
It's bald

ROCK
Mr. Custer

TV
Joe

MOVIES
El Cid

MAGAZINES
TV Guide

Popular Culture 53

BOOKS
What children's book is about Flopsy, Mopsy, Cottontail, and Peter?

ADVERTISING
The copy read, "Dispense with a Horse," and it was the first-ever ad for a car. Not surprisingly, the Winton Motor Car Co. ad ran in what magazine?

ROCK
Whose first hit was "Born to Run"?

TV
What two series featured Richard Anderson as Oscar Goldman?

MOVIES
In what state was the restaurant where Humphrey Bogart took his hostages in *The Petrified Forest*?

MAGAZINES
What industry does the trade magazine *The Hollywood Reporter* cover?

Popular Culture 54

BOOKS
What historic event prompted Norman Mailer to write *The Naked and the Dead*?

ADVERTISING
What product was named for the creator's brother-in-law, Dr. Joshua Vick?

ROCK
What white-faced rockers had a platinum album named *Shout at the Devil* in 1984?

TV
What is James Adams better known as?

MOVIES
What was Gentle Ben in the Disney film of the same name?

MAGAZINES
What magazine produced the Chevy Chase film vehicle, *Vacation*?

Answers: Popular Culture 53

BOOKS
The Tale of Peter Rabbit by Beatrix Potter

ADVERTISING
Scientific American

ROCK
Bruce Springsteen

TV
The Six Million Dollar Man and *The Bionic Woman*

MOVIES
Arizona

MAGAZINES
Entertainment

Answers: Popular Culture 54

BOOKS
The bombing of Pearl Harbor

ADVERTISING
Vick's VapoRub

ROCK
Motley Crue

TV
Grizzly Adams

MOVIES
A brown bear

MAGAZINES
National Lampoon

Popular Culture 55

BOOKS
What is the pen name of Charles Lutwidge Dodgson?

ADVERTISING
"What becomes a legend most?" was the slogan for what product?

ROCK
Cass Elliott, John Phillips, and Michelle Phillips were three members of the Mamas and Papas. Who was the fourth?

TV
What 1983 prime-time series was cancelled and then renewed as a result of audience demand?

MOVIES
What baseball player did William Bendix play in 1948?

MAGAZINES
What famous clown had his own comic book from 1970–71?

Popular Culture 56

BOOKS
Which one of these was not written by Pierre Boulle? (a) *Enderby* (b) *The Bridge Over the River Kwai* (c) *Planet of the Apes*

ADVERTISING
When you call, "Hey, Culligan Man," you need a remedy for: (a) dirty laundry (b) hard water (c) spotty glasses

ROCK
Who hit it big with "The Banana Boat Song" in 1957?

TV
Was it *Dan Raven* or *Dan August* that starred Burt Reynolds?

MOVIES
What film took place in and around the 1903 St. Louis World's Fair?

MAGAZINES
John Leonard was one in a long line of editors-in-chief for what recently revived magazine?

BOOKS
Lewis Carroll

ADVERTISING
Blackglama Mink

ROCK
Dennis Doherty

TV
Cagney and Lacey

MOVIES
Babe Ruth

MAGAZINES
Ronald McDonald

Answers: Popular Culture 56

BOOKS
a) *Enderby*

ADVERTISING
b) hard water

ROCK
Harry Belafonte

TV
Dan August

MOVIES
Meet Me in St. Louis

MAGAZINES
Vanity Fair

Popular Culture 57

BOOKS
Fear of Flying was Erica Jong's first novel. What was her second?

ADVERTISING
What first-of-its-kind company did businessman Volney Palmer found in Philadelphia, PA in 1841?

ROCK
In what city is the House of the Rising Sun?

TV
What popular sixties series drew its name from an African word for *doctor*?

MOVIES
True or false: Peter Sellers played more than one role in Stanley Kubrick's classic film, *Dr. Strangelove*.

MAGAZINES
Gloria Steinem co-founded what woman's magazine?

Popular Culture 58

BOOKS
What was the name of Edith Wharton's tragic heroine in *The House of Mirth*?

ADVERTISING
What color is Johnnie Walker's jacket?

ROCK
Name the two Allman brothers.

TV
Episodes of what series were edited together to make feature-length films entitled *The Karate Killers* and *How to Steal the World*, among others?

MOVIES
Name the detective played by William Powell in the Thin Man movies.

MAGAZINES
What is the name of the Elaine Powers's fitness magazine?

BOOKS
How to Save Your Own Life

ADVERTISING
An ad agency

ROCK
New Orleans

TV
Daktari

MOVIES
True

MAGAZINES
Ms.

BOOKS
Lily Bart

ADVERTISING
Red

ROCK
Gregg and Duane

TV
The Man from U.N.C.L.E.

MOVIES
Nick Charles

MAGAZINES
Feeling Great

Popular Culture 59

BOOKS
What author and statesman, later beheaded, wrote *Utopia*?

ADVERTISING
Who, in the 1930s, promised to make you a new man using "Dynamic Tension"?

ROCK
Who derived his famous nickname from his first hit song, "The Fat Man"?

TV
What popular British import stars John Cleese as a hotel owner named Basil?

MOVIES
Which one of these horror characters did Boris Karloff play? (a) Dracula   (b) the Wolfman   (c) the Mummy

MAGAZINES
How much does *Playboy* pay for jokes sent in by its readers?

Popular Culture 60

BOOKS
Who wrote *Le Mort D'Arthur*?

ADVERTISING
In the 1940s, which one of these was not a Lee garment brand?   (a) Lee Union-Alls   (b) Lee Navy Blues   (c) Lee Army Twills

ROCK
With what Doors song did Jose Feliciano climb the charts in 1968?

TV
Who played the young Kunta Kinte in *Roots*?

MOVIES
The Philadelphia Story, starring Cary Grant and Katharine Hepburn, was based on a Broadway play of the same title by what playwright?

MAGAZINES
What magazine is famous for its Norman Rockwell cover paintings?

BOOKS
Sir Thomas More

ADVERTISING
Charles Atlas

ROCK
Fats Domino

TV
Fawlty Towers

MOVIES
c) The Mummy

MAGAZINES
$50

Answers: Popular Culture 60

BOOKS
Malory (Sir Thomas)

ADVERTISING
b) Lee Navy Blues

ROCK
"Light My Fire"

TV
LeVar Burton

MOVIES
Philip M. Barry

MAGAZINES
The Saturday Evening Post

Popular Culture 61

BOOKS
Who wrote the thirty-two novels in the nineteenth century's enormously popular Waverly series?

ADVERTISING
"Two of the most famous names in America sleep together." Larry Hagman is one of the names; what's the other?

ROCK
Under what name did Marie McDonald McLaughlin record "To Sir With Love"?

TV
What is the name of the farmer character on "Captain Kangaroo?"

MOVIES
What instrument did Robin Williams play in *Moscow on the Hudson*?

MAGAZINES
What magazine is commonly referred to as "GQ"?

Popular Culture 62

BOOKS
Which Peter Benchley tale is about honeymooners swept up in intrigue in Bermuda?

ADVERTISING
What does IBM stand for?

ROCK
What pop singer starred in the movie, "Goodbye, Mr. Chips?"

TV
Name the three original female leads of *Charlie's Angels*.

MOVIES
What Jane Fonda film prophetically anticipated the Three Mile Island accident?

MAGAZINES
What turn-of-the-century magazine publisher was eulogized by one paper as having "contributed to journalism the talent of a meat packer, the morals of a moneychanger, and the manner of an undertaker"?

BOOKS
Sir Walter Scott

ADVERTISING
Cannon Mills

ROCK
Lulu

TV
Mr. Green Jeans

MOVIES
Saxophone

MAGAZINES
Gentlemen's Quarterly

Answers: Popular Culture 62

BOOKS
The Deep

ADVERTISING
International Business Machines

ROCK
Petula Clark

TV
Kate Jackson, Jaclyn Smith, and Farrah Fawcett

MOVIES
The China Syndrome

MAGAZINES
Frank A. Munsey

Popular Culture 63

BOOKS
Which one of the Apollo XI astronauts did *not* write a book?

ADVERTISING
True or false: The name Kodak derives from Kinetic Optical Device and the initials of its inventor.

ROCK
What rock star made his big-screen debut in the flop film *Hard To Hold*?

TV
Who were Linc, Julie, and Pete?

MOVIES
In what film did Sissy Spacek immortalize the life of country music star Loretta Lynn?

MAGAZINES
What subject is covered in the popular fan magazine, *Trek*?

Popular Culture 64

BOOKS
The author of the best-seller *Medusa and The Snail* is (a) Stephen Jay Gould (b) John McPhee (c) Lewis Thomas

ADVERTISING
What product inspired national paranoia with the line, "Even your best friends won't tell you"?

ROCK
How far were Brewer and Shipley "Over the Line"?

TV
Spell the full surname of Detective "Wojo" of *Barney Miller*.

MOVIES
Name the popular 1981 rehash of the legend of King Arthur.

MAGAZINES
What magazine forms the basis of Larry Flynt's publishing empire?

BOOKS
Neil Armstrong

ADVERTISING
False. It's a nonsense word that means nothing.

ROCK
Rick Springfield

TV
The Mod Squad

MOVIES
Coal Miner's Daughter

MAGAZINES
Star Trek

Answers: Popular Culture 64

BOOKS
c) Lewis Thomas

ADVERTISING
Listerine

ROCK
"One Toke"

TV
Wojohowicz

MOVIES
Excalibur

MAGAZINES
Hustler

Popular Culture 65

BOOKS
To what John Steinbeck novel is his *Sweet Thursday* a sequel?

ADVERTISING
What kind of complexion did Palmolive promise to help women keep?

ROCK
Whose first hit was *Maybellene* in 1956?

TV
What show's theme song was "Danny Boy"?

MOVIES
Was it *Caravans, Cavern,* or *Cavalcade* that was based on a James Michener novel?

MAGAZINES
How much does *Moviegoer* magazine cost?

Popular Culture 66

BOOKS
Which one of these was not written by Truman Capote? (a) *Ancient Evenings* (b) *Breakfast at Tiffany's* (c) *Music for Chameleons*

ADVERTISING
Accent, the "flavor enhancer," is made from what vegetable?

ROCK
What did Adam Ant barely advocate we do in the title cut of his 1983 album?

TV
What motion picture legend came to the small screen in *The Smith Family*?

MOVIES
What role has been played by both Judy Garland and Diana Ross?

MAGAZINES
What is the "National Business and Financial Weekly"?

BOOKS
Cannery Row

ADVERTISING
Schoolgirl

ROCK
Chuck Berry

TV
Make Room for Daddy, aka *The Danny Thomas Show*

MOVIES
Caravans

MAGAZINES
It's free, handed out at movie theaters nationwide

BOOKS
a) *Ancient Evenings*

ADVERTISING
The sugar beet

ROCK
Strip

TV
Henry Fonda

MOVIES
Dorothy in *The Wizard of Oz*

MAGAZINES
Barron's

Popular Culture 67

BOOKS
What popular attorney was introduced in Erle Stanley Gardner's *The Case of the Velvet Claws*?

ADVERTISING
What food staple "helps build strong bodies twelve different ways"?

ROCK
What group did Eddie Kendricks leave in May, 1971, to launch a solo career?

TV
What sleuthing brothers were played by Shaun Cassidy and Parker Stevenson?

MOVIES
Who was the first actor to portray JFK on the screen?

MAGAZINES
What magazine is bordered in yellow?

Popular Culture 68

BOOKS
Who wrote *The Decameron*?

ADVERTISING
How was Canada Dry's flop 1960s soft drink, Sport Cola, ahead of its time?

ROCK
What kind of "Yell" does Billy Idol sing about?

TV
In what series, based on a hit film, did Christopher Connelly and Jodie Foster play father and daughter?

MOVIES
What is the top-grossing film of all time?

MAGAZINES
How frequently is *Life* magazine published?

BOOKS
Perry Mason

ADVERTISING
Wonder Bread

ROCK
The Temptations

TV
The Hardy Boys

MOVIES
Cliff Robertson, in *PT 109*

MAGAZINES
National Geographic

Answers: Popular Culture 68

BOOKS
Giovanni Boccaccio

ADVERTISING
It was caffeine-free

ROCK
"Rebel"

TV
Paper Moon

MOVIES
E.T., the Extraterrestrial

MAGAZINES
Monthly

Popular Culture 69

BOOKS
What is Mary O'Hara's enduring novel about horsing around?
ADVERTISING
What product was named after the Gators, the University of Florida football team?
ROCK
How many miles did Otis Redding roam in *Sitting on the Dock of the Bay*?
TV
What is Bullwinkle Moose's middle initial?
MOVIES
What famous G-man appeared as himself in *The F.B.I. Story*?
MAGAZINES
True or false: *Prime Time* Magazine is about television.

Popular Culture 70

BOOKS
What historical event is the setting for *The Scarlet Pimpernel*?
ADVERTISING
What beer's slogan was, "Who is the ale man? He could be *you*, the man with a thirst for a manlier brew."
ROCK
What are the last names of David, Stephen, Graham, and Neil?
TV
Which one of Popeye's eyes is permanently shut?
MOVIES
Who played Jim Bowie to John Wayne's Davy Crockett?
MAGAZINES
What is the name of Time, Inc.'s science magazine?

BOOKS
My Friend Flicka

ADVERTISING
Gatorade

ROCK
Two thousand

TV
J.

MOVIES
J. Edgar Hoover

MAGAZINES
False. It's about living and loving when you're over forty.

Answers: Popular Culture 70

BOOKS
The French Revolution

ADVERTISING
Ballantine

ROCK
Crosby, Stills, Nash & Young

TV
The right

MOVIES
Richard Widmark

MAGAZINES
Discover

Popular Culture 71

BOOKS
What literary character was inspired by Queen Goosefoot, the mother of Charlemagne?

ADVERTISING
Which one of the following was not a 1960s snack food?   (a) Wowees   (b) Funyons   (c) Sesame Sillys

ROCK
The music from what motion picture gave instrumentalist Deodato his biggest hit?

TV
Name the four Nelsons who dominated the airwaves from 1952–1966.

MOVIES
Which one of these actors did not play Jesus Christ?   (a) Max von Sydow   (b) Charlton Heston   (c) Jeffrey Hunter

MAGAZINES
Which of the following magazines is *not* a Condé Nast publication?   (a) *Town and Country*   (b) *Glamour*   (c) *Better Homes and Gardens*

Popular Culture 72

BOOKS
Which one of the following is not one of the Brothers Karamazov?   (a) Ivan   (b) Feodor   (c) Dmitri

ADVERTISING
What was "the one and only cereal that comes in the shape of animals"?

ROCK
According to Cyndi Lauper, what "Changes Everything"?

TV
What kind of animals do the aliens look like in *V*?

MOVIES
What is Indiana Jones's favorite weapon?

MAGAZINES
Name the magazine whose departments include "Around the Mall" and "The View from the Castle."

Answers: Popular Culture 71

BOOKS
Mother Goose

ADVERTISING
a) Wowees

ROCK
2001: A Space Odyssey

TV
Ozzie, Harriet, David, and Eric ("Ricky")

MOVIES
b) Charlton Heston

MAGAZINES
a) *Town and Country*

Answers: Popular Culture 72

BOOKS
b) Feodor is the father Karamazov

ADVERTISING
Crispy Critters

ROCK
"Money"

TV
Lizards

MOVIES
A bullwhip

MAGAZINES
Smithsonian

Popular Culture 73

BOOKS
Which one of these celebrities' autobiographies was not called *My Story*? (a) Mike Douglas (b) Kareem Abdul-Jabbar (c) Ingrid Bergman

ADVERTISING
What company's mascot is Elsie the Cow?

ROCK
What was the name of the band consisting of Ginger Baker, Jack Bruce, and Eric Clapton?

TV
What 1969–70 NBC series was based on the works of James Thurber?

MOVIES
Name the 1978 movie in which Gregory Peck plays the villainous Nazi Josef Mengele.

MAGAZINES
Name the artist/publisher of *Interview*.

Popular Culture 74

BOOKS
What island is the setting for *The Teahouse of the August Moon*?

ADVERTISING
What does Patricia Neal recommend for people who want to "fight pain and win"?

ROCK
Name the lead singer of the Blue Notes.

TV
Who co-anchored the ABC evening news with Barbara Walters?

MOVIES
Which one of the following heroes did muscleman Gordon Scott *not* play? (a) Hercules (b) Tarzan (c) John Henry

MAGAZINES
What is "Young America's Favorite Magazine"?

Answers: Popular Culture 73

BOOKS
b) Kareem Abdul-Jabbar

ADVERTISING
Borden

ROCK
Cream

TV
My World and Welcome to It

MOVIES
The Boys from Brazil

MAGAZINES
Andy Warhol

Answers: Popular Culture 74

BOOKS
Okinawa

ADVERTISING
Anacin

ROCK
Harold Melvin

TV
Harry Reasoner

MOVIES
c) John Henry

MAGAZINES
Seventeen

Popular Culture 75

BOOKS
Who wrote "If," one of the world's most popular poems?

ADVERTISING
True or false: Pall Mall cigarettes were named for a ritzy London street.

ROCK
From what state does Johnny B. Goode hail?

TV
What ex-alien played Paris on *Mission: Impossible*?

MOVIES
True or false: Bela Lugosi played Dracula more often than any other actor.

MAGAZINES
What is "The Magazine for Today's Black Woman"?

Popular Culture 76

BOOKS
What book, arguably the most incendiary of the nineteenth century, was subtitled "Life Among the Lowly"?

ADVERTISING
What product didn't you use if you were "Often a bridesmaid, never a bride"?

ROCK
What was the stage name of 1960s star Joe McDonald?

TV
What mid-1960s series was about Tim O'Hara and his unusual Uncle Martin?

MOVIES
What was the relationship of opposing lawyers Katharine Hepburn and Spencer Tracy in *Adam's Rib*?

MAGAZINES
"Window Seat" and "Travel & Money" are departments of what magazine?

BOOKS
Rudyard Kipling

ADVERTISING
True

ROCK
Louisiana

TV
Leonard Nimoy

MOVIES
False. He played the Count twice, Christopher Lee nine times.

MAGAZINES
Essence

BOOKS
Uncle Tom's Cabin

ADVERTISING
Listerine

ROCK
Country Joe

TV
My Favorite Martian

MOVIES
They were wife and husband

MAGAZINES
Travel & Leisure

Popular Culture 77

BOOKS
Who wrote the play *Under Milk Wood*?

ADVERTISING
"I'd rather fight than switch" was the slogan for what cigarette?

ROCK
Who wrote "Leader of the Pack"?

TV
What was the first name of Grandpa Walton?

MOVIES
Who was nominated for the Best Supporting Actress Oscar in *Silkwood*?

MAGAZINES
What was the name of the magazine that Gene Barry published in the TV series *The Name of the Game?*

Popular Culture 78

BOOKS
Who created Tarzan of the Apes?

ADVERTISING
Sea Dog is the pet of what breakfast cereal headliner?

ROCK
What male superstar recorded duets with Kim Carnes, Sheena Easton, and Dolly Parton?

TV
What was Chief Thunderthud's favorite expression?

MOVIES
Who played Clark Gable in the 1976 film *Gable and Lombard*?

MAGAZINES
What is the only magazine whose title begins with an apostrophe?

BOOKS
Dylan Thomas

ADVERTISING
Tarryton

ROCK
Ellie Greenwich

TV
Zeb

MOVIES
Cher

MAGAZINES
People

BOOKS
Edgar Rice Burroughs

ADVERTISING
Cap'n Crunch

ROCK
Kenny Rogers

TV
Kowa Bunga

MOVIES
James Brolin

MAGAZINES
'Teen

Popular Culture 79

BOOKS
What is the name of the award handed out by the Science Fiction Writers of America?

ADVERTISING
What was the "champagne of bottle beer"?

ROCK
Was it Jackie Lee, Michele Lee, or Leapy Lee who had a hit in 1965 with *The Duck*?

TV
In what series did Lee Marvin play Lieutenant Frank Ballinger?

MOVIES
Who conducted the score for *Fantasia*?

MAGAZINES
What do the initials of the magazine *RCM* stand for?

Popular Culture 80

BOOKS
Who is Edmond Dantes?

ADVERTISING
Which toilet tissue claims to be as soft as cotton?

ROCK
Name the two singers on the 1984 hit, "Tell Me I'm Not Dreamin'"

TV
What was the occupation of *The Greatest American Hero*?

MOVIES
To what position was James Earl Jones promoted in *The Man*?

MAGAZINES
Name the Peterson magazine that presents the coveted "Car of the Year" award.

BOOKS
The Nebula

ADVERTISING
Miller

ROCK
Jackie Lee

TV
M Squad

MOVIES
Leopold Stokowski

MAGAZINES
Radio Control Modeler

Answers: Popular Culture 80

BOOKS
The Count of Monte Cristo

ADVERTISING
Cottonelle

ROCK
Jermaine and Michael Jackson

TV
High school teacher

MOVIES
President of the United States

MAGAZINES
Motor Trend

Popular Culture 81

BOOKS
Who wrote the Kent Family Chronicles?

ADVERTISING
What does L.S./M.F.T. stand for?

ROCK
Whose biggest hit was *Downtown*?

TV
Who was president during the time of *The Wild, Wild West*?

MOVIES
In what 1977 film did Art Carney and Lily Tomlin team up to solve a murder?

MAGAZINES
Name the publication whose regular departments include "The 19th Hole" and "Scorecard."

Popular Culture 82

BOOKS
Michael Korda told readers of his best-seller how to get and how to use . . . what?

ADVERTISING
True or false: Cigarettes may no longer be advertised in magazines as of January 1, 1985.

ROCK
What punctuation mark did Rudy Martinez use as his stage name when he sang with the Mysterians?

TV
What police drama had eight million stories to tell?

MOVIES
In 1983, *Never Say Never Again* marked the return of what actor to what role?

MAGAZINES
What is "more than a magazine . . . a way of life"?

Answers: Popular Culture 81

BOOKS
John Jakes

ADVERTISING
Lucky Strike Means Fine Tobacco

ROCK
Petula Clark

TV
Ulysses S. Grant

MOVIES
The Late Show

MAGAZINES
Sports Illustrated

Answers: Popular Culture 82

BOOKS
Power

ADVERTISING
False

ROCK
The question mark

TV
Naked City

MOVIES
Sean Connery as James Bond

MAGAZINES
The Mother Earth News

Popular Culture 83

BOOKS
Whose towering work, first published in 1755, was *Dictionary of the English Language*?

ADVERTISING
Madge, the manicurist, is the spokesperson for which dishwashing product?

ROCK
What piece of furniture fails to hear Neil Diamond's cry, "I am ... I said."

TV
Who plays *Dynasty*'s Alexis?

MOVIES
In what 1983 film does Peter O'Toole star as a drunken actor on the loose in New York?

MAGAZINES
Which magazine carries the regular feature "The Talk of the Town"?

Popular Culture 84

BOOKS
Which one of these lands or peoples was not visited by Lemuel Gulliver?   (a) Houyhnhnms   (b) Mu   (c) Glubbdubdrib

ADVERTISING
Who printed the first metallic newspaper advertisement?

ROCK
Name the Michael Jackson album that preceded *Thriller*.

TV
What TV character was nicknamed Rinty?

MOVIES
Who was Fay Wray's tallest, darkest leading man?

MAGAZINES
What was the first magazine to print a 3-D picture in its pages?

Answers: Popular Culture 83

BOOKS
Samuel Johnson

ADVERTISING
Palmolive

ROCK
The chair

TV
Joan Collins

MOVIES
My Favorite Year

MAGAZINES
The New Yorker

Answers: Popular Culture 84

BOOKS
b) Mu

ADVERTISING
Reynolds.

ROCK
Off the Wall

TV
Rin-Tin-Tin

MOVIES
King Kong

MAGAZINES
Look magazine, in 1963

Popular Culture 85

BOOKS
Name the book journalist Lowell Thomas wrote about his experiences with T. E. Lawrence in Arabia.

ADVERTISING
What is "footman" Dr. Scholl's first name?

ROCK
According to a Beatles song, how many days are there in a week?

TV
What long-running game show required contestants to match prizes on the flip side of numbered squares?

MOVIES
Who is the shark's last victim in *Jaws*?

MAGAZINES
What is the leading magazine for fans of Dungeons and Dragons role-playing games?

Popular Culture 86

BOOKS
What is the name of Jean Anouilh's play about Henry II's problems with the Archbishop of Canterbury?

ADVERTISING
True or false: Ford's Model T was so-named because so much of it was made of tin.

ROCK
In 1959, Elvis Presley sang about a "Big Hunk o'"... what?

TV
Which one of these rock groups was *not* turned into a Saturday morning cartoon series? (a) The Jackson Five (b) The Beatles (c) Kiss

MOVIES
Who was James Bond's first screen enemy?

MAGAZINES
The letters column of what magazine is called "Readers Afield"?

Answers: Popular Culture 85

BOOKS
With Lawrence in Arabia

ADVERTISING
William

ROCK
Eight

TV
Concentration

MOVIES
Quint

MAGAZINES
Dragon

Answers: Popular Culture 86

BOOKS
Becket

ADVERTISING
False. It was the model he produced after the *S*.

ROCK
"Love"

TV
c) Kiss

MOVIES
Dr. No.

MAGAZINES
Sports Afield

Popular Culture 87

BOOKS
Which city is the setting of John Hersey's *The Wall*? (a) Warsaw (b) Berlin (c) Shanghai

ADVERTISING
In 1734, Joseph Broome was the first of his vanishing breed in America to take out a newspaper advertisement. What was he?

ROCK
Whose first solo hit was "Mother and Child Reunion"?

TV
"I hate meeces to pieces" was the motto of what TV cat?

MOVIES
Name the three theatrical movies that have titles one letter long.

MAGAZINES
What was the first magazine to publish a hologram on its cover?

Popular Culture 88

BOOKS
What did Dick Gregory call his autobiography so that whenever the word was uttered it would advertise his book?

ADVERTISING
What cigarette urged, "Take a puff—it's springtime!"

ROCK
Cher sang about "Gypsies, Tramps, and"...what?

TV
What was the spaceship of *Tom Corbett, Space Cadet*?

MOVIES
Who was Errol Flynn's most frequent co-star, making eight films with the swashbuckler?

MAGAZINES
What is the world's largest numismatic publication?

Answers: Popular Culture 87

BOOKS
a) Warsaw

ADVERTISING
A magician

ROCK
Paul Simon

TV
Jinks

MOVIES
M, Q, Z

MAGAZINES
National Geographic

Answers: Popular Culture 88

BOOKS
Nigger

ADVERTISING
Salem

ROCK
Thieves

TV
The *Polaris*

MOVIES
Olivia de Havilland

MAGAZINES
Coinage

Popular Culture 89

BOOKS
What Johnny Gruelle character did little Marcella find in her grandmother's attic?

ADVERTISING
What was "more than a camera, it's almost alive! It's only nineteen dollars and ninety-five"?

ROCK
True or false: Rick Dees and His Cast of Idiots had a big hit in 1976 with "Disco Delilah."

TV
In what state is Andy Griffith's Mayberry located?

MOVIES
What Edna Ferber story became a film classic starring Elizabeth Taylor, Rock Hudson, and James Dean?

MAGAZINES
What is the name of the pictorial feature on the last page of *Life*?

Popular Culture 90

BOOKS
Who is the famous Dr. "A," who wrote *The Sensuous Dirty Old Man*?

ADVERTISING
What was the "Cream-Oil Hair Tonic"?

ROCK
Where was it "Raining" for Buddy Holly?

TV
Who played CPO Otto Sharkey?

MOVIES
What was Abbott and Costello's first starring movie?

MAGAZINES
What is "The Magazine for Growing Companies"?

Answers: Popular Culture 89

BOOKS
Raggedy Ann

ADVERTISING
The Polaroid Swinger

ROCK
False. It was "Disco Duck."

TV
North Carolina

MOVIES
Giant

MAGAZINES
"Miscellany"

Answers: Popular Culture 90

BOOKS
Isaac Asimov

ADVERTISING
Wildroot

ROCK
"In My Heart"

TV
Don Rickles

MOVIES
Buck Privates

MAGAZINES
Inc.

Popular Culture 91

BOOKS
Which one of these was not a published spoof of *Jonathan Livingston Seagull*? (a) *Ludwig von Wolfgang Vulture* (b) *Livingston Ipresume Crow* (c) *Jonathan Segal Chicken*

ADVERTISING
What company introduced the first home microwave oven, the Radarange, in 1967?

ROCK
Whose first hit was "Snowbird" in 1970?

TV
On what show are there characters named Grandfather Clock and Bunny Rabbit?

MOVIES
What infamous event is recounted in *Tora! Tora! Tora!*?

MAGAZINES
What is the official magazine of Broadway theatergoers?

Popular Culture 92

BOOKS
Who wrote *The Teachings of Don Juan: A Yaqui Way of Knowledge*?

ADVERTISING
What product is associated with the line, "There's a man in the bathtub!"

ROCK
Who recorded the album *Tapestry*?

TV
Which one of these theatrical films did *not* inspire a TV series? (a) *Bob & Carol & Ted & Alice* (b) *Major Dundee* (c) *Logan's Run*

MOVIES
What edifice does Citizen Kane build for his wife?

MAGAZINES
Which one of these humor magazines was co-edited by Gloria Steinem? (a) *Help* (b) *Up Your Nose and Out Your Ear* (c) *Sick*

Answers: Popular Culture 91

BOOKS
b) *Livingston Ipresume Crow*

ADVERTISING
Amana

ROCK
Anne Murray

TV
Captain Kangaroo

MOVIES
The attack on Pearl Harbor

MAGAZINES
Playbill

Answers: Popular Culture 92

BOOKS
Carlos Castaneda

ADVERTISING
Mr. Bubble

ROCK
Carole King

TV
b) *Major Dundee*

MOVIES
An opera house

MAGAZINES
a) *Help*

Popular Culture 93

BOOKS
What Shirley Jackson chiller is about Eleanor Vance's adventures in a haunted house?

ADVERTISING
What "bleaches out tough food stains better than any other leading cleanser"?

ROCK
What are the first names of singers Hall and Oates?

TV
What was the name of Crusader Rabbit's tiger sidekick?

MOVIES
Who played Paul Newman's son in 1984's misfire, *Harry and Son*?

MAGAZINES
What children's digest is named after a famous egg?

Popular Culture 94

BOOKS
Which one of these is not a character in *Everyman*?   (a) Five-Wits   (b) Good-Deeds   (c) Prudence

ADVERTISING
Madge manicured her clients while they soaked their fingers in what?

ROCK
Levi Stubbs, Duke Fakir, Obie Benson, and Lawrence Payton are the members of what top group?

TV
Who played Robin to Adam West's Batman?

MOVIES
Sigourney Weaver was the only human survivor in what 1979 science-fiction thriller?

MAGAZINES
What magazine always features an obituary on its last page?

Answers: Popular Culture 93

BOOKS
The Haunting of Hill House

ADVERTISING
Comet

ROCK
Daryl and John

TV
Rags

MOVIES
Robby Benson

MAGAZINES
Humpty Dumpty

Answers: Popular Culture 94

BOOKS
c) Prudence

ADVERTISING
Palmolive dishwashing liquid

ROCK
The Four Tops

TV
Burt Ward

MOVIES
Alien

MAGAZINES
Rolling Stone

Popular Culture 95

BOOKS
Men Against the Sea was part two of what sprawling trilogy?

ADVERTISING
"Your baby's comfort begins with" . . . what?

ROCK
Who is known as "The Divine Miss M"?

TV
Whose theme song boasted that this cartoon character was known "from the Atlantic to the Pacific"?

MOVIES
Who was Burt Lancaster's commanding officer in *Run Silent, Run Deep*?

MAGAZINES
What magazine selects "The Man of the Year"?

Popular Culture 96

BOOKS
Who is P. L. Travers's most famous literary creation?

ADVERTISING
In what make of car did Dinah Shore encourage you to "see the U.S.A."?

ROCK
What singer's first hit was *It's Not Unusual*?

TV
What show moved from New York to Southern California in 1972?

MOVIES
What movie ominously advertised itself as being about a place "where nothing could go worng"? (sic)

MAGAZINES
What German publication ran the bogus Hitler diaries in 1983?

Answers: Popular Culture 95

BOOKS
The Bounty Trilogy

ADVERTISING
Luvs

ROCK
Bette Midler

TV
Tom Terrific

MOVIES
Clark Gable

MAGAZINES
Time

Answers: Popular Culture 96

BOOKS
Mary Poppins

ADVERTISING
Chevrolet

ROCK
Tom Jones

TV
The Tonight Show

MOVIES
Westworld

MAGAZINES
Stern

Popular Culture 97

BOOKS
Name the best-selling nonfiction book by author/astronomer Carl Sagan.

ADVERTISING
"They said it couldn't be done—they said nobody could do it." But what cigarette all of a sudden had "more taste to it"?

ROCK
How many "Miles High" was the 1966 Byrds hit?

TV
Who provided the voice for the "sock puppet" Lamb Chops?

MOVIES
True or false: Both *The Godfather* and *The Godfather, Part II* won the Best Picture Oscar.

MAGAZINES
What is the in-flight publication of American Airlines?

Popular Culture 98

BOOKS
Who wrote the monumental *The History of the Decline and Fall of the Roman Empire*?

ADVERTISING
What product was named for its chief component, muriate of berberine?

ROCK
What group backed Tommy James?

TV
What sitcom, a *Maude* spinoff, followed the lives of Florida, James, and J J Evans?

MOVIES
Who played Doctor Detroit?

MAGAZINES
What distinction is held by *Funnies on Parade*?

BOOKS
Cosmos

ADVERTISING
L & M

ROCK
"Eight"

TV
Shari Lewis

MOVIES
True

MAGAZINES
American Way

Answers: Popular Culture 98

BOOKS
Edward Gibbon

ADVERTISING
Murine

ROCK
The Shondells

TV
Good Times

MOVIES
Dan Aykroyd

MAGAZINES
It was the first comic book

Popular Culture 99

BOOKS
What is the subject of Harlan Ellison's *The Glass Teat*?

ADVERTISING
"What puts *you* in the picture?" was the slogan of what movie process?   (a) 3-D   (b) CinemaScope   (c) Cinerama

ROCK
What city did Dionne Warwick sing about in 1968?

TV
Duke Slater was the best friend of what marine?

MOVIES
Whose last film was 1980's *The Hunter*?

MAGAZINES
What is the top selling magazine of pop-psychology?

Popular Culture 100

BOOKS
To what book was *Gods from Outer Space* the follow-up?

ADVERTISING
Who once advertised his wares by placing a six-story-tall electric pickle in New York's Times Square?

ROCK
Who had a huge hit in 1964 with the instrumental "Java"?

TV
The theme song of what series insisted, "We're the young generation, and we've got something to say"?

MOVIES
What event was targeted by terrorists in *Black Sunday*?

MAGAZINES
What magazine annually awards the "Arkies"?

Answers: Popular Culture 99

BOOKS
TV

ADVERTISING
c) Cinerama

ROCK
San Jose

TV
Gomer Pyle

MOVIES
Steve McQueen

MAGAZINES
Psychology Today

Answers: Popular Culture 100

BOOKS
Chariots of the Gods

ADVERTISING
Henry J. Heinz

ROCK
Al Hirt

TV
The Monkees

MOVIES
The Super Bowl

MAGAZINES
Electronic Games

PART TWO

THE DECADES

The Decades 1

40s
What important journal was found in Amsterdam following the Second World War?

50s
How many presidents were elected during the fifties?

60s
Which Academy Award-winning movie about two misfits was originally rated X?

70s
Who was court-martialed in 1971 for atrocities in Southeast Asia?

80s
In what state did the pope and Ronald Regan meet in May, 1984?

FUTURE
What term is derived from "cybernetic organism"?

The Decades 2

40s
In what year was Korea split in two?

50s
Name the two Rosenbergs executed for treason.

60s
What Nobel Prize-winning author shot himself to death in 1961?

70s
What state did Gerald Ford represent in Congress before being promoted?

80s
What company unveiled the disappointing PCjr?

FUTURE
What phrase is used to describe the climatic change that atomic warfare will bring?

Answers: The Decades 1

40s
The Diary of Anne Frank

50s
One (Eisenhower)

60s
Midnight Cowboy

70s
Lieutenant William Calley

80s
Alaska

FUTURE
Cyborg

Answers: The Decades 2

40s
1948

50s
Julius and Ethel

60s
Ernest Hemingway

70s
Michigan

80s
IBM

FUTURE
Nuclear Winter

The Decades 3

40s
On what day of the week was Pearl Harbor bombed?
50s
Name the Italian liner that went down in 1956.
60s
What animal did the Yippies run for president in 1968?
70s
For what post was Harrold Carswell rejected?
80s
Name the Ohio senator who made an aborted bid for the presidency in 1984?
FUTURE
What is the next planet the *Voyager* spacecraft are scheduled to encounter?

The Decades 4

40s
Who coined the phrase "Iron Curtain"?
50s
Name the pope elected in 1958.
60s
What was the name of the "doorway" between the divided Berlins?
70s
What year was the bicentennial?
80s
What president's centennial birthday was celebrated in 1984?
FUTURE
In what year will the 21st century's first presidential election be held?

Answers: The Decades 3

40s
Sunday

50s
Andrea Doria

60s
A pig

70s
Supreme Court Justice

80s
John Glenn

FUTURE
Uranus

Answers: The Decades 4

40s
Winston Churchill

50s
John XXIII

60s
Checkpoint Charlie

70s
1976

80s
Harry S. Truman

FUTURE
2000

The Decades 5

40s
What newspaper ran the infamous headline "Dewey Defeats Truman"?

50s
Who did George Jorgensen become?

60s
What disastrous military maneuver did the U.S. back in 1961?

70s
What became the capital of the reunited North and South Vietnam?

80s
What craze included terms like "hand glide" and "back slide"?

FUTURE
According to trends of the past decade, which of these fuels will remain the *least* popular source of power?   (a) coal   (b) petroleum   (c) natural gas

---

The Decades 6

40s
In what island group is Corregidor, which fell to the Japanese in 1942?

50s
Name the first atomic submarine.

60s
In what city was the 1968 Democratic Convention held?

70s
Haile Selassie was ousted as the ruler of what nation in 1974?

80s
What country's elections pit José Napoleon Duarte against Roberto D'Aubuisson?

FUTURE
True or false: It is not expected that machine intelligence will surpass that of humans within the next one hundred years.

Answers: The Decades 5

40s
The Chicago Daily Tribune

50s
Christine Jorgensen

60s
The Bay of Pigs Invasion

70s
Hanoi

80s
Breakdancing

FUTURE
a) coal

Answers: The Decades 6

40s
The Philippines

50s
The *Nautilus*

60s
Chicago

70s
Ethiopia

80s
El Salvador

FUTURE
False

The Decades 7

40s

From what nation did Sri Lanka (then Ceylon) gain its independence in 1948?

50s

What lamp reached its height of popularity in the late 50s?

60s

What was the centerpiece of the Seattle World's Fair?

70s

What did Gerald Ford's flop acronym, W.I.N., stand for?

80s

Name the first man to ride the space shuttle into orbit twice.

FUTURE

What scientific venture did Ronald Reagan call for in his 1984 State of the Union address?

The Decades 8

40s

The body of what World War II leader was hung upside down in public?

50s

What British king died in 1952?

60s

Name the London street that rose to prominence in the fashion-conscious 1960s.

70s

What was the name of the Russian spacecraft that linked with an *Apollo* module in 1975?

80s

Whose visit to South Korea in May, 1984, promoted the tightest security in that nation's history?

FUTURE

According to George Orwell, what familial member is watching us?

Answers: The Decades 7

40s
Great Britain

50s
The pole lamp

60s
The Space Needle

70s
Whip Inflation Now

80s
John Young

FUTURE
A permanently inhabited space station

Answers: The Decades 8

40s
Benito Mussolini

50s
George VI

60s
Carnaby

70s
Soyuz

80s
Pope John Paul II

FUTURE
Big Brother

The Decades 9

40s

What world leader did his generals attempt to kill by bomb in 1943?

50s

The Ford Motor Company has never lived down the failure of what car, introduced in the 1950s?

60s

True or false: Hubert Humphrey ran against JFK in the 1960 presidential primaries.

70s

In 1974, what became the world's tallest building?

80s

What was the flight number of the Korean airliner shot down by a Soviet fighter in 1983?

FUTURE

By 1990, what percentage of office workers is expected to be using data or word-processing hardware?   (a) 50%   (b) 75%   (c) 90%

The Decades 10

40s

What was the nickname of Nazi general Erwin Rommel?

50s

Name the political group established in 1950 by H. N. Arrowsmith, Jr.

60s

Which Kennedy family member survived the crash of a private plane?

70s

What revolutionary group clubbed Steven Weed with a bottle in February, 1974, while abducting his girl friend?

80s

What brand of sweetener did G. D. Searle & Co. put on the market in 1983?

FUTURE

What does SETI hope to find in the near future?

Answers: The Decades 9

40s
Adolf Hitler

50s
The Edsel

60s
True

70s
The Sears Tower

80s
007

FUTURE
50%

Answers: The Decades 10

40s
"The Desert Fox"

50s
The American Nazi Party

60s
Ted Kennedy

70s
The Symbionese Liberation Army

80s
NutraSweet

FUTURE
Extraterrestrial intelligence

The Decades 11

40s

What two world leaders met in Casablanca in 1943?

50s

How many stars were on the American flag in 1958?

60s

What was the better-known name of the decade's most famous model, Lesley Hornby?

70s

What major American city defaulted on its debts in 1978?

80s

What major comic book character underwent a costume change in 1984, wearing threads that were black and white instead of blue and red?

FUTURE

The Planetary Society is actively engaged in setting up college courses to grapple with the problem of what space objective?

The Decades 12

40s

What was the code name of Germany's long-planned but never executed invasion of England?

50s

Established in 1953, NASA stands for what?

60s

Name the Rockefeller who went to New Guinea and never returned.

70s

What woman won the Nobel Prize in 1979?

80s

Who was the famous space companion of astronauts John Fabian and Rick Hauck?

FUTURE

According to Stansfield Turner, former CIA director, what will be more important in the future than "adding speed or maneuverability" to military aircraft?

40s
Churchill and Roosevelt

50s
Forty-eight

60s
Twiggy

70s
Cleveland

80s
The Amazing Spider-Man

FUTURE
Colonizing Mars

Answers: The Decades 12

40s
Operation Sea Lion

50s
National Aeronautics and Space Administration

60s
Michael

70s
Mother Teresa

80s
Sally Ride

FUTURE
The effectiveness of its missiles

The Decades 13

40s
Who was the winning general at El Alamein?
50s
What plastic staple was first introduced in 1952?
60s
Who were the first astronauts to fly the two-occupant *Gemini* capsule?
70s
What was the number of the proposition backed by Howard Jarvis of California?
80s
With what nation's military did the U.S. conduct desert maneuvers in 1981?
FUTURE
What is fast replacing office size as the preferred executive status symbol?

The Decades 14

40s
What noted pacifist was assassinated in 1948?
50s
What Russian word, popularized in the late 1950s, means "fellow wayfarer"?
60s
What was the fourth nation to explode an atom bomb?
70s
What nation tried the Gang of Four?
80s
The U.S. mining of what nation's harbors created a congressional uproar in April, 1984?
FUTURE
What is rapidly outstripping the singles bar as *the* place to meet people?

Answers: The Decades 13

40s
Montgomery

50s
The bank credit card

60s
Gus Grissom and John Young

70s
13

80s
Egypt

FUTURE
Original art

Answers: The Decades 14

40s
Mahatma Gandhi

50s
Sputnik

60s
China

70s
China

80s
Nicaragua

FUTURE
The health club

The Decades 15

40s
What was Jeanette Rankin the only member of Congress to vote against in 1941?

50s
Where did the unoccupied Soviet spacecraft *Lunik* journey?

60s
In what state did the Beatles land when they first came to the United States?   (a) California   (b) Maryland   (c) New York

70s
What did Cesar Chavez urge Americans to boycott in 1970?

80s
True or false: The Federal government's 1983 deficit exceeded a quarter of a trillion dollars.

FUTURE
What will be returning to our celestial neighborhood in 1986?

The Decades 16

40s
What did the infamous letters HUAC stand for?

50s
True or false: President Eisenhower suffered a heart attack in 1958.

60s
What was the first *Apollo* mission to carry a color TV camera to the moon?

70s
Name the senator who presided at the Watergate hearings.

80s
In what state was Claus von Bulow prosecuted?

FUTURE
What does the future-time designation "AF" stand for in *Brave New World*?

119

40s
A declaration of war against Japan

50s
To the moon

60s
c) New York

70s
Lettuce

80s
False. It weighed in at just over $180 billion.

FUTURE
Halley's Comet

Answers: The Decades 16

40s
House Un-American Activities Committee

50s
False. It happened in 1954.

60s
Apollo XII

70s
Sam Ervin

80s
Rhode Island

FUTURE
After Ford

The Decades 17

40s
Whose regime did the U.S. fail to recognize when it was established in 1949?

50s
What European nation suffered a short-lived revolution in 1956?

60s
In what European city was Martin Luther King, Jr.'s assassin apprehended?

70s
What Georgia city did Jimmy Carter put on the map?

80s
Who was Constable Yvonne Fletcher?

FUTURE
What year has Deng Xiaoping set for the completion of his plan to make China "a modern country"?

The Decades 18

40s
True or false: Albert Einstein became an American citizen in 1940.

50s
What world leader proclaimed in 1957, "U.S. imperialism is a paper tiger"?

60s
In what area of the Dallas police station did Jack Ruby shoot Lee Harvey Oswald?   (a) garage   (b) basement   (c) lobby

70s
Where was the Queen Elizabeth when it caught fire and sank in 1972?

80s
What was the name of Jesse Jackson's hoped-for coalition?

FUTURE
According to a 1983 survey, what animal will soon surpass dogs as the most frequent victims of hit-and-run driving?

Answers: The Decades 17

40s
Mao Tse-tung's

50s
Hungary

60s
London

70s
Plains

80s
The British policewoman killed by a sniper at the Libyan Embassy in April, 1984.

FUTURE
2000

Answers: The Decades 18

40s
True

50s
Mao Tse-tung

60s
b) basement

70s
Hong Kong

80s
Rainbow Coalition

FUTURE
Squirrels

The Decades 19

40s

What late general captured Rome in 1944?

50s

In 1953, who briefly interrupted David Ben-Gurion's tenure as Israel's Prime Minister?

60s

What popular tranquilizer was introduced in 1963?

70s

In what hit film did Barbra Streisand portray a nice Jewish girl married to a beautiful Gentile boy?

80s

By 1983, fewer than 10% of all the movie theaters in America had only one of these.

FUTURE

According to a 1975 film, what will replace warfare?

The Decades 20

40s

What clandestine government agency was founded in 1947?

50s

Whose hands—all that TV audiences ever saw—did the Kefauver hearings make famous?

60s

True or false: New York was the most populous state in 1962.

70s

What did the Canadian Parliament adopt for the nation in 1965?

80s

What was the bug that caused havoc in California?

FUTURE

Big banks, the traditional pioneers in office automation, are about to be outspent in this area by what market?

Answers: The Decades 19

40s
Mark Clark

50s
Moshe Sharett

60s
Valium

70s
The Way We Were

80s
A screen

FUTURE
Rollerball

Answers: The Decades 20

40s
The Central Intelligence Agency

50s
Frank Costello's

60s
True

70s
A new flag

80s
The Mediterranean fruit fly

FUTURE
City governments

The Decades 21

40s
Who died at Warm Springs, GA, in 1945?

50s
What is the informal name of Richard Nixon's famous 1952 speech?

60s
In what city was Martin Luther King, Jr., assassinated in 1968?

70s
Who was the first native American to be canonized by the Catholic church?

80s
True or false: Iran invaded Iraq in 1981.

FUTURE
The most powerful earthquake in North America's future is not expected to come from the San Andreas Fault but from what Midwestern fault?

The Decades 22

40s
From what nation did Iceland liberate itself in 1944?

50s
Konrad Adenauer was Chancellor of what nation?

60s
In 1968, what became the fifth nation to have "the bomb"?

70s
Who was the target of would-be assassin Arthur Bremer?

80s
What sport did Robert Redford play in the 1984 film *The Natural*?

FUTURE
The extinction of the dinosaurs is theorized to have been caused by what event, which is due to recur tens of millions of years hence?

Answers: The Decades 21

40s
Franklin Roosevelt

50s
The Checkers Speech

60s
Memphis, TN

70s
Mother Seton

80s
False. The reverse is true.

FUTURE
The New Madrid Fault

Answers: The Decades 22

40s
Denmark

50s
West Germany

60s
France

70s
George Wallace

80s
Baseball

FUTURE
Collision between earth and a comet

The Decades 23

40s
What nation was born in May of 1948?
50s
What conflagration was started when troops moved south across the 38th parallel?
60s
How was war criminal Adolf Eichmann put to death?
70s
What popular TV mini-series was based on an Irwin Shaw novel?
80s
Who was shot dead at the airport in Manila, the Philippines, in 1983?
FUTURE
True or False: For a short time after death, hair and nails will continue to grow.

The Decades 24

40s
What was the name of JFK's older brother, killed during World War II?
50s
What was the book written by the *Mercury* astronauts?
60s
Which nations combined to form Tanzania?
70s
Name the war hero who quit the Israeli cabinet in 1979.
80s
President Reagan was shot in 1981 as he left what hotel?
FUTURE
CETI is the acronym for what foreseen event?

40s
Israel

50s
The Korean War

60s
He was hanged

70s
Rich Man, Poor Man

80s
Benigno Aquino

FUTURE
True

40s
Joe

50s
We Seven

60s
Tanganyika and Zanzibar

70s
Moshe Dayan

80s
The Washington Hilton

FUTURE
Communication with Extraterrestrial Intelligence

The Decades 25

40s

Who was elected president of Argentina in 1946?

50s

Anastasio Somoza, assassinated in 1956, was president of what country?

60s

From what country did Malta win their freedom in 1964? (a) France (b) England (c) Italy

70s

What caused Iceland and England to sever diplomatic relations in 1976?

80s

What corporation was granted over one billion dollars in government loans?

FUTURE

Is it nuclear fission or fusion scientists hope to achieve to obtain cheap, minimal-hazard power?

The Decades 26

40s

Mount Suribachi, site of a famous American flag-raising, is located where?

50s

What statesman won the 1953 Nobel Prize for literature?

60s

What was the first nation ever to resign from the United Nations?

70s

Name the Cambodian leader who ended years of exile by returning to his country in 1975.

80s

Which one of these is *not* a space-faring shuttle? (a) Challenger (b) Enterprise (c) Discovery

FUTURE

What is the theoretically feasible Dyson Sphere intended to encircle?

40s
Juan Peron

50s
Nicaragua

60s
b) England

70s
Cod-fishing rights

80s
Chrysler

FUTURE
Fusion

40s
On Iwo Jima

50s
Winston Churchill

60s
Indonesia

70s
Prince Sihanouk

80s
b) *Enterprise*—it flew only in earth's atmosphere

FUTURE
A sun or star

The Decades 27

40s
What did Mohammed Reza Pahlavi become in 1941?

50s
Whom did General Matthew Ridgway replace in 1951 as Supreme Commander, Allied Powers?

60s
What New York City arts complex was opened in the mid-1960s?

70s
Name the Denton, TX, lady who became Miss America in 1971.

80s
What group was compensated in 1981 with just over five thousand dollars per person for their unusual stint overseas?

FUTURE
Scientists hope to use the DNA of the intestinal bacterium *Escherichia coli* to mass-produce what anti-virus chemical?

The Decades 28

40s
The landing at what Italian beach in 1944 so infuriated Hitler that he ordered "radical surgery" to remove the Allied forces?

50s
What three nations formed the United Arab States in 1958?

60s
What did French Togoland become in 1960?

70s
What syndicated columnist and former *Good Morning America* commentator won the Pulitzer Prize in 1972 for national reporting?

80s
In 1981, a nuclear reactor in Iraq was razed by fighters from what country?

FUTURE
What form of asexual reproduction has yet to produce a human being?

40s
Shah of Iran

50s
General Douglas MacArthur

60s
Lincoln Center

70s
Phyllis George

80s
The Iranian hostages

FUTURE
Interferon

Answers: The Decades 28

40s
Anzio

50s
Yemen, Egypt, and Syria

60s
The Republic of Togo

70s
Jack Anderson

80s
Israel

FUTURE
Cloning

The Decades 29

40s

What New York political figure was Miss America of 1945?

50s

Prophetically, President Eisenhower sent U.S. troops to what nation in 1958, in an effort to help establish a new government?

60s

What kind of overcoat did John F. Kennedy wear for his inauguration?

70s

Who ousted Milton Obote as an African power in 1971?

80s

Upon which hand does Michael Jackson wear his famous glove?

FUTURE

What is the name of the British Interplanetary Society's highly publicized study that proposes sending a nuclear pulse rocket through interstellar space?

The Decades 30

40s

What exiled Russian revolutionary was slain in 1940?

50s

Why was King Talal of Jordan ousted and succeeded by his son Hussein?

60s

What city's art treasures were hardest hit by the floods that ravaged Italy in 1966?

70s

What exiled religious leader, living in France, returned home in 1979?

80s

In April, 1983, the U.S. embassy in what city was destroyed, killing more than fifty people?

FUTURE

True or false: If you age like Merlin, you will get younger as you grow older.

40s
Bess Myerson

50s
Lebanon

60s
He wore no overcoat.

70s
Idi Amin

80s
His right hand

FUTURE
Project Daedalus

Answers: The Decades 30

40s
Leon Trotsky

50s
He was insane.

60s
Florence

70s
Ayatollah Khomeini

80s
Beirut

FUTURE
True: Merlin ages backward, each year growing younger.

The Decades 31

40s
What famous "14" made science news in 1947?

50s
Name the belts that made news when they were found in 1958.

60s
Complete this anti-war chant: "Hell, no . . ."

70s
True or false: In the last decade, the nonwhite population of South Africa had the highest percentage of "accidental deaths" of any people on earth.

80s
In the movie *Terms of Endearment,* Emma makes love to husband Flap to what romantic tune?

FUTURE
Dye injected into certain areas of the body, and destructive laser light absorbed *only* by tissue containing that color, is being tested against what disease?

The Decades 32

40s
By executive order, what did President Truman ban from the army in 1948?

50s
How did the 22nd Amendment, ratified in 1951, affect the presidency?

60s
Discovered in 1967, pulsating radio sources in space are better known as what?

70s
The troops of what two nations entered Cambodia in 1970?

80s
Seven people died after popping what cyanide-spiked medicine?

FUTURE
A space colony located at Lagrange points L-4 and L-5 would be closest to what body of the Solar System?   (a) Earth   (b) the moon   (c) the sun

40s
The development of carbon-14 dating

50s
The Van Allen radiation belts

60s
"... we won't go!"

70s
True

80s
"Gee, Officer Krupke" from *West Side Story*

FUTURE
Cancer

Answers: The Decades 32

40s
Segregation

50s
The tenure of office was limited to two terms.

60s
Pulsars

70s
The U.S. and South Vietnam

80s
Extra-strength Tylenol

FUTURE
b) the moon

The Decades 33

40s

What two nations declared war on the U.S. on December 11, 1941?

50s

What two powerful unions merged in 1955?

60s

Name the U.S. Navy intelligence ship seized by North Korea in 1968.

70s

How did the 26th amendment affect the way Americans vote?

80s

For what act did John Paul II forgive Memet Ali Agca?

FUTURE

Scientists fear that the burning of fossil fuels will cause what "effect" to permanently heat up Earth?

The Decades 34

40s

Did Japan, Germany, or Italy surrender on May 7, 1945?

50s

In 1956, a national uproar developed after seamstress Rosa Parks refused to give what to a white man in Montgomery?

60s

Name the first black appointed to the Supreme Court.

70s

What government did the U.S. recognize in 1979?

80s

In 1983, Anne Burford left her position as the administrator of what agency?

FUTURE

According to Thomas More's *Utopia*, the workday of the future will be how many hours long?   (a) 3   (b) 6   (c) 10

Answers: The Decades 33

40s
Germany and Italy

50s
AF of L and CIO

60s
The *Pueblo*

70s
Eighteen-year-olds were allowed to cast ballots.

80s
Shooting Pope John Paul II

FUTURE
The greenhouse effect

Answers: The Decades 34

40s
Germany

50s
Her seat on a bus

60s
Thurgood Marshall

70s
The People's Republic of China

80s
The Environmental Protection Agency

FUTURE
b) 6

The Decades 35

40s

What conference was held in 1945 to determine the occupation and settlement of Europe?

50s

The Arkansas National Guard was called in to prevent the integration of schools in what city?

60s

In 1962, after campus bloodshed, who became the first black to attend the University of Mississippi?

70s

The Watergate burglars were caught in what office?

80s

Fireworks attended the Brooklyn Bridge's celebration of what birthday?   (a) 50th   (b) 75th   (c) 100th

FUTURE

Which world-famous structure will be 100 years old in 2031?   (a) The Empire State Building   (b) The United Nations Building   (c) The Eiffel Tower

---

The Decades 36

40s

The Lend-Lease Act enabled friendly nations to procure what American product free of charge?

50s

Name the ursine ecologist introduced in 1950.

60s

What was the only monochromatic Beatles album?

70s

Name the famous Idaho dam that went to pieces in 1976.

80s

Name the Reagan who ran for political office in 1982.

FUTURE

According to the Office of Technology Assessment, Americans will be using 150 million of these by the year 2000.

40s
The Potsdam Conference

50s
Little Rock, Arkansas

60s
James H. Meredith

70s
Democratic Party national headquarters

80s
c) 100th

FUTURE
a) The Empire State Building

Answers: The Decades 36

40s
Weapons

50s
Smokey the Bear

60s
The White Album

70s
The Teton River Dam

80s
Maureen

FUTURE
Automobiles

The Decades 37

40s
The Communist nations enacted Cominform in response to what postwar U.S. undertaking?

50s
Who became President of France in 1958?

60s
What international do-gooders' organization did JFK establish in 1961?

70s
Who was Gerald Ford's running mate in 1976?

80s
Which of Jimmy Carter's cabinet members resigned because of the ill-fated rescue attempt of the American hostages in Iran?

FUTURE
What average is due to increase from 19.4 to 24.6 per gallon by the turn of the century?

The Decades 38

40s
Which one of these is the official name of East Germany? (a) German Democratic Republic (b) Federal Republic of Germany (c) Peoples' State of Germany

50s
Premier Khrushchev used the 20th Communist Party Congress in Moscow to initiate what Russian program?

60s
Indira Gandhi, who became the prime minister of India in 1966, was related to what other Indian political figure?

70s
Kent State University, the site of four student deaths during a 1970 antiwar protest, is located in what state?

80s
Who was elected to the French presidency in 1981?

FUTURE
According to Plato, what must kings become before a perfect society can be achieved? (a) slaves (b) philosophers (c) poets

40s
Marshall Plan

50s
Charles De Gaulle

60s
The Peace Corps

70s
Robert Dole

80s
Cyrus Vance (Secretary of State)

FUTURE
Miles per gallon an automobile will travel

Answers: The Decades 38

40s
a) German Democratic Republic

50s
De-Stalinization

60s
Jawaharlal Nehru

70s
Ohio

80s
Francois Mitterand

FUTURE
b) philosophers

The Decades 39

40s

Whose government fled to Taiwan in 1949?

50s

Of what nation did Ngo Dinh Diem become premier in 1955?

60s

What Communist leader was ousted in 1964?

70s

What mastermind behind the "Cultural Revolution" died in 1976?

80s

Name the company Mary Cunningham and William Agee put in the news.

FUTURE

What resilient and populous class of animals do scientists concede would inherit the earth after an all-out nuclear war?

The Decades 40

40s

In 1947, what northern dominion became independent from India?

50s

What nation was divided at the 17th parallel in 1954?

60s

What was crossed for the first time on foot in 1968–69?

70s

Lon Nol became the leader of what nation in 1970? (a) Cambodia (b)Thailand (c) Laos

80s

San Franciscans attempted to oust what mayor in 1983?

FUTURE

Because of orbital peculiarities, which planet is and will remain the outermost planet for years to come?

40s
Chiang Kai-shek

50s
South Vietnam

60s
Nikita Khrushchev

70s
Mao Tse-tung

80s
Bendix

FUTURE
Insects

Answers: The Decades 40

40s
Pakistan

50s
Vietnam

60s
The North Pole

70s
a) Cambodia

80s
Dianne Feinstein

FUTURE
Neptune

The Decades 41

40s
The U.S. granted what islands their independence in 1946?

50s
Not satisfied with climbing the world's tallest mountain, who crossed Antarctica during 1955–58?

60s
Patrice Lumumba was premier of what African republic?

70s
What did East Pakistan become after a devastating civil war?

80s
In what nation did a Soviet submarine find itself beached in 1981?

FUTURE
What word is most often used in tandem with the possibility of splicing DNA?

The Decades 42

40s
Who did Marshal Badoglio follow to power in 1943?

50s
What was the first ship to cross the North Pole under water?

60s
In 1960, Archbishop Makarios became the first president of what republic?

70s
What world leader died in Cairo in 1970?

80s
Which nation booted Abolhassan Banisadr from the presidency in 1981?

FUTURE
To what planet is the *Galileo* space probe slated to go?

40s
The Philippines

50s
Edmund Hillary

60s
The Congo

70s
Bangladesh

80s
Sweden

FUTURE
Recombination (recombinant)

Answers: The Decades 42

40s
Benito Mussolini

50s
The *Nautilus*

60s
Cyprus

70s
Gamal Abdel Nasser

80s
Iran

FUTURE
Jupiter

The Decades 43

40s
What commission did the U.S. establish in 1946, which hadn't been needed two years before?

50s
Where did Premier Khrushchev and President Eisenhower meet in 1959?

60s
How many presidential children called the White House home during this decade?

70s
To what nation did the U.S. cede the Canal Zone in 1979?

80s
How many numbers did the post office add to every zip code?

FUTURE
Alex and his "droogs" are future-time thugs in what Anthony Burgess novel?

The Decades 44

40s
What city was bombed in a 1942 air raid led by James H. Doolittle?

50s
What was the name of the most famous political dog of this decade?

60s
What section of Los Angeles was plagued by race riots in 1965?

70s
In 1977, Jimmy Carter made what issue the cornerstone of his foreign policy?

80s
In 1981, two war planes from what nation were shot down in the Mideast by American fighters?

FUTURE
True or false: Iran will have the capacity to produce an atom bomb before the end of the decade.

40s
The Atomic Energy Commission

50s
At Camp David

60s
Six. John John and Caroline Kennedy, Lucy and Lynda Johnson, and Julie and Tricia Nixon.

70s
Panama

80s
Four

FUTURE
A Clockwork Orange

Answers: The Decades 44

40s
Tokyo

50s
Nixon's dog, Checkers.

60s
Watts

70s
Human rights

80s
Libya

FUTURE
True

The Decades 45

40s
Luis Munoz Marin was the first elected governor of what U.S. territory?

50s
What was the first nation established with the help of the U.N.?

60s
What enlightening device did Theodore Maiman demonstrate for the first time in 1960?

70s
Who was the first American to walk on the moon in this decade?

80s
Who preceded George Shultz as Secretary of State?

FUTURE
True or false: The moon is slowly approaching Earth.

The Decades 46

40s
What clothing item did a five-star general and future president of the United States popularize?

50s
What did Jonas Salk develop in 1954?

60s
What did cardiac specialist Michael De Bakey use for the first time during surgery in 1963?

70s
What did Patrick Steptoe and Robert Edwards "father" in England in 1978?

80s
What company introduced the "Walkman"?

FUTURE
What poet said that the world will end "not with a bang but with a whimper"?

40s
Puerto Rico

50s
Libya

60s
The laser

70s
Alan B. Shepard, Jr.

80s
Alexander Haig

FUTURE
False. It is receding.

Answers: The Decades 46

40s
The Eisenhower jacket

50s
The polio vaccine

60s
An artificial heart

70s
The first test-tube baby

80s
Sony

FUTURE
T. S. Eliot

The Decades 47

40s
What factor was discovered in 1940?

50s
In 1954, Sir Grantley Adams became the first prime minister of what West Indies island republic?

60s
What popular hat style did Jackie Kennedy begin with her inauguration bonnet?

70s
From what nation did Angola win its independence in 1975?

80s
Who is honored by the newly created national holiday that will be observed for the first time on the first Monday of January, 1986?

FUTURE
On what day of the week will January 1, 2000 fall?

The Decades 48

40s
In World War II, did Brazil side with the Axis or the Allies?

50s
Before there was a Timmy, another little boy owned Lassie. What was his name?

60s
True or false: Algeria declared war on Israel in 1967 but sent no troops into battle.

70s
Since 1979, all proper names from what nation have been spelled according to the Pinyan system of English translation?

80s
Name the Warner Communications hi-tech division that went from megabuck-maker to liability in the first three years of the decade.

FUTURE
What does Arthur C. Clarke prophesy we will *finally* be able to control by the year 2020?

40s
Rh

50s
Barbados

60s
The pillbox

70s
Portugal

80s
Martin Luther King, Jr.

FUTURE
Saturday

Answers: The Decades 48

40s
The Allies

50s
Jeff

60s
True

70s
China

80s
Atari

FUTURE
The weather

The Decades 49

40s
To what did Siam change its name in 1949?

50s
True or false: In 1955, the position assumed by Sam Rayburn for the third time was Speaker of the House.

60s
Who carried five Southern states in the 1968 presidential election?

70s
Name the Ugandan airport attacked by Israeli commandoes.

80s
What was the principal reason given by the Soviet Union for dropping out of the 1984 Summer Olympics?

FUTURE
When is the next leap year?

The Decades 50

40s
Where did Marshal Pétain form his government after France fell to Germany?

50s
What European principality gained a princess in 1956?

60s
Name the Middle Eastern organization formed in 1964 to establish a homeland for its people.

70s
In 1978, more than nine hundred people died in the name of what cult, based in Jonestown, Guyana?

80s
In 1983, Harold Washington was elected mayor of what city?

FUTURE
Who would have been seventy years old in 1987?   (a) John F. Kennedy   (b) Marilyn Monroe   (c) James Dean

Answers: The Decades 49

40s
Thailand

50s
True

60s
George C. Wallace

70s
Entebbe

80s
Lack of security

FUTURE
1988

Answers: The Decades 50

40s
Vichy

50s
Monaco

60s
The Palestine Liberation Organization

70s
The People's Temple

80s
Chicago

FUTURE
a) John F. Kennedy

The Decades 51

40s

True or false: Liechtenstein sided with the Axis during World War II.

50s

Name the Russian author who won the Nobel Prize for literature in 1958.

60s

What musical, about a former New York mayor, won the Pulitzer Prize in 1960?

70s

What team did baseball's Washington Senators become in 1972?

80s

In 1984, what became the top-selling record album of all time?

FUTURE

What novel predicts the rise of a simian empire over the ruins of our own?

The Decades 52

40s

True or false: Albert Einstein won a Nobel Prize in physics for his contributions to the atom bomb.

50s

What did the European Economic Community establish in 1957 in the name of political unity?

60s

How many members were in the group The Dave Clark Five?

70s

In 1971, what nation was admitted to the U.N., and what nation was ousted?

80s

What celebrated figures were wed in St. Paul's Cathedral?

FUTURE

In what year will the U.S. celebrate its second sesquicentennial?

40s
False. It was neutral.

50s
Boris Pasternak

60s
Fiorello!

70s
The Texas Rangers

80s
Thriller (Michael Jackson)

FUTURE
Planet of the Apes

Answers: The Decades 52

40s
False

50s
The Common Market

60s
Five

70s
Communist China; Taiwan

80s
Prince Charles and Lady Diana Spencer

FUTURE
2076

The Decades 53

40s
What term was Franklin Roosevelt serving when the decade began?

50s
True or false: John F. Kennedy won a Nobel Prize in 1957.

60s
In the comic book series *Archie*, what were the names of Archie's two girlfriends?

70s
Who claimed that American builders like to "take paradise and put up a parking lot"?

80s
What "sting" operation nabbed New Jersey Senator Harrison A. Williams?

FUTURE
The drug Minoxidil is being tested as a cure to curb what bodily loss?

The Decades 54

40s
How many nuclear bombs were dropped on civilian targets in this decade?

50s
Who held the heavyweight boxing title as this decade came to a close?

60s
What team joined baseball in 1962?

70s
What rock opera was made into a film in 1973?

80s
True or false: Jimmy Carter, Rosalynn Carter, and Billy Carter all published memoirs in the first half of this decade.

FUTURE
Which one of these future-oriented magazines is *not* extinct?   (a) *Future Life*   (b) *Next*   (c) *The Planetary Report*

Answers: The Decade 53

40s
His second

50s
False. He won a Pulitzer Prize.

60s
Veronica and Betty

70s
Joni Mitchell

80s
Abscam

FUTURE
Baldness

Answers: The Decades 54

40s
Two (Hiroshima and Nagasaki)

50s
Ingemar Johansson

60s
The New York Mets

70s
Jesus Christ Superstar

80s
False. Billy did not.

FUTURE
c) *The Planetary Report*

The Decades 55

40s
What team won the most World Series during this decade?

50s
What pact was signed by the Soviet Union and its Eastern European allies?

60s
A 1967 coup in what country forced King Constantine II into exile?

70s
What was the name of Mario Puzo's post-*Godfather* best-seller?

80s
Prince Andrew visited the set of what motion picture during his 1984 American tour?

FUTURE
How far in the future does the *Star Wars* saga take place?

The Decade 56

40s
Who wrote the novels *A Tree Grows In Brooklyn* and *Tomorrow Will Be Better?*

50s
According to the Tuskegee Institute, 1952 was the first year no black suffered from this crime.

60s
This bridge, the largest suspension bridge in the U.S., was completed in 1964.

70s
What unharmonious statistic jumped from less than ten percent at the turn of the century to more than half in this decade?

80s
What hot product was produced by Apollo, Telysys, and Data Age—and drove them swiftly into bankruptcy?

FUTURE
The science of bionics is devoted to: (a) simulating living systems with machinery   (b) generating new tissue   (c) creating machines with human emotions.

40s
The New York Yankees (four)

50s
The Warsaw Pact

60s
Greece

70s
Fools Die

80s
2010: Odyssey Two

FUTURE
It doesn't. It takes place "A long time ago...."

Answers: The Decades 56

40s
Betty Smith

50s
Lynching

60s
The Verrazano Narrows Bridge (New York)

70s
The number of married couples getting divorced

80s
Videogames

FUTURE
a) simulating living systems with machinery

The Decades 57

40s

What future first lady was married to Warren C. Williams from 1942–47?

50s

HUD head Robert Weaver was the first black ever to reach what level of government?

60s

Who was sentenced to 99 years in prison in 1969?

70s

Where in the Canary Islands did two jumbo jets collide on the runway, resulting in 579 fatalities?

80s

What city called in a psychic to help solve the murders of nearly thirty children?

FUTURE

Project Cyclops is a program designed to place radio telescopes where?

The Decades 58

40s

What nation annexed Lithuana in 1941?

50s

Which one of these posts did Earl Warren *not* hold?   (a) governor   (b) chief justice   (c) vice-president

60s

What murder victim made headlines when New Yorkers watched from their window as she was killed—and didn't call the police?

70s

What presidential library was opened in Cambridge, MA?

80s

Which one of these cities has *not* had a woman mayor?   (a) Houston   (b) Philadelphia   (c) Chicago

FUTURE

True or false: Celestially speaking, Earth's sun is still considered a "baby" star.

40s
Betty Ford

50s
Cabinet level

60s
James Earl Ray

70s
Tenerife

80s
Atlanta

FUTURE
On the moon

Answers: The Decades 58

40s
Russia

50s
c) vice-president

60s
Kitty Genovese

70s
John F. Kennedy's

80s
b) Philadelphia

FUTURE
False. It's approximately halfway to oblivion.

The Decades 59

40s

To what famous crooner was Nancy Barbato married during this decade?

50s

What is William Golding's 1955 novel about a group of boys stranded on an island after a plane crash?

60s

This *Pretty Baby* actress and Michael Jackson escort was born in 1965.

70s

This Ugandan capital was in the news in 1979 when invading Tanzanian troops came within fifty miles of it.

80s

Name the two New York political titans who published books in 1984.

FUTURE

In which H. G. Wells novel is the future governed by tyrannical Morlocks?

The Decades 60

40s

True or false: No Oscars were presented from 1941–45 because gold for the statuettes was too costly.

50s

Name the selfless Alsatian doctor, missionary, and musician who won the Nobel Peace prize in 1952.

60s

What Theodore H. White book about the presidency won the Pulitzer Prize in 1962?

70s

What airline owned the plane that crashed as it took off from Chicago in 1979, putting a hex on DC-10s?

80s

How much did it cost to send a first-class letter as the decade dawned?

FUTURE

When aliens one day discover the interstellar *Pioneer 10* and *11* spacecraft, they will find a plaque with two human figures wearing what?

Answers: The Decades 59

40s
Frank Sinatra

50s
Lord of the Flies

60s
Brooke Shields

70s
Kampala

80s
New York City mayor Ed Koch and New York governor Mario Cuomo.

FUTURE
The Time Machine

Answers: The Decades 60

40s
False

50s
Albert Schweitzer

60s
The Making of the President 1960

70s
American Airlines

80s
Fifteen cents

FUTURE
Nothing

The Decades 61

40s
Wilhelm Gustloff, Joo Maru, and *General Steuben* all suffered what fate during this decade?

50s
True or false: More Americans fought in the Korean War than in Vietnam.

60s
Vonda Kay Van Dyke and Debra Dene Barnes were among ten of these in the 1960s.

70s
At the close of the decade, on what was Procter & Gamble outspending its nearest rival by $200 million?

80s
Having accumulated nearly nine million books by 1980, what public library is the largest in the nation?

FUTURE
When space farers reach Alpha Centauri in the far future, what change will they notice in the constellation Cassiopeia?

The Decades 62

40s
True or false: World War II did not officially end, by presidential proclamation, until December, 1946.

50s
Name the pilot who won a Pulitzer Prize in 1954 for a book he wrote.

60s
What former resident of Russia and the U.S. became a world leader in 1969?

70s
In 1973, who became Los Angeles's first black mayor?

80s
What is the only nation that has more Communist Party members than the Soviet Union?

FUTURE
What term has been coined for the eventual transformation of inhospitable worlds into habitable ones?

Answers: The Decades 61

40s
They sank; all were boats

50s
True

60s
Miss Americas

70s
TV advertising

80s
The New York Public Library

FUTURE
Our sun will be one of the stars in it.

Answers: The Decades 62

40s
True

50s
Charles A. Lindbergh

60s
Golda Meir

70s
Tom Bradley

80s
Communist China

FUTURE
Terraforming

The Decades 63

40s
Name the feminist and novelist who died in 1941, leaving behind such works as *Mrs. Dalloway* and *To the Lighthouse*.

50s
What famous Harvard educated poet and lawyer died in 1955?

60s
Which one of these was *not* a series of lunar probes launched by NASA in the 1960s? (a) *Ranger* (b) *Surveyor* (c) *Copernicus*

70s
True or false: A leftist uprising in Managua, Nicaragua, in 1972, left ten thousand people dead and spawned the present-day hostilities.

80s
How many days did the 1982 football strike last? (a) 31 (b) 57 (c) 79

FUTURE
True or false: Approximately four billion years from now, the earth will boil and Mars will become earthlike.

The Decades 64

40s
In 1945, a bomber plowed into the top of what famous landmark, causing many deaths and extensive destruction?

50s
What movie craze began in 1953 and ended in 1954?

60s
What athlete earned the nickname "Doctor" because of the number of college scholarships he was offered?

70s
Now Mrs. Bernie Shaw, what was this woman's name when she was pardoned by President Carter in 1979?

80s
What Chicago-based TV star published his best-selling autobiography in 1980?

FUTURE
According to many scientists, what terrestrial cataclysm never ended but is merely in a comparatively brief period of remission?

Answers: The Decades 63

40s
Virginia Woolf

50s
Wallace Stevens

60s
c) *Copernicus*

70s
False. An earthquake was responsible for the deaths.

80s
b) 57

FUTURE
True

Answers: The Decades 64

40s
The Empire State Building

50s
3-D

60s
Julius Erving (Dr. J)

70s
Patty Hearst

80s
Phil Donahue

FUTURE
The Ice Age

The Decades 65

40s
Who married divorced dancer Betty Bloomer in 1948?

50s
After forty years, skull fragments from what "caveman" were proved to be a hoax?

60s
Who became Mrs. David Eisenhower in 1968?

70s
Who was named Secretary-General of the United Nations in 1971?

80s
Name the past and present presidents of the Screen Actors' Guild who repeatedly went head-to-head over political matters.

FUTURE
According to Carl Sagan, what celestial phenomenon may one day be used as a means of moving quickly through time and across the galaxies?

The Decades 66

40s
What Boston nightclub burned down in 1942, killing nearly five hundred people?

50s
Who defeated Helen Gahagan Douglas for a Senate seat in 1950 after a singularly vicious campaign?

60s
Name the UCLA philosophy instructor who was fired because she admitted to being a Communist.

70s
What political odd couple shared the Nobel Peace Prize in 1978?

80s
What profession does Lech Walesa practice?

FUTURE
What will be celebrated on October 12, 1992?

40s
Gerald Ford

50s
Piltdown man

60s
Julie Nixon

70s
Kurt Waldheim

80s
Ed Asner and Charlton Heston

FUTURE
Black holes

Answers: The Decades 66

40s
The Cocoanut Grove

50s
Richard Nixon

60s
Angela Davis

70s
Menachem Begin and Anwar el Sadat

80s
He's an electrician

FUTURE
The 500th anniversary of Columbus's arrival in America

The Decades 67

40s

What play about a rabbit won the Pulitzer Prize in 1945?

50s

In 1951, 200,000 were left homeless as Kansas and Missouri were hit by the worst natural disaster of what kind in U.S. history?

60s

To what position was Giovanni Battista Cardinal Montini elevated in 1963?

70s

What four-letter screen game gave birth to the videogame industry in 1972?

80s

Name the building outside of which John Lennon was shot.

FUTURE

Name the 1936 film that erroneously predicted that a second "Great War" would drag on for decades.

The Decades 68

40s

What was the first film to win Best Picture in this decade?

50s

The staggering popularity of what comedian caused NBC to sign him to a thirty-year contract?

60s

What AFL quarterback was pro football's leading passer in 1964 and 1966?

70s

What Milwaukee Bucks player started the decade by being named Rookie of the Year?

80s

What infamous Bob Guccione film finally came to videocassette in 1984?

FUTURE

According to legend, who will return at some future time if needed to save England from disaster?

40s
Harvey

50s
Floods

60s
Pope

70s
Pong

80s
The Dakota

FUTURE
Things to Come

Answers: The Decades 68

40s
Rebecca

50s
Milton Berle

60s
Len Dawson

70s
Lew Alcindor (Kareem Abdul-Jabbar)

80s
Caligula

FUTURE
King Arthur

40s

What coiffure term was derived in the 1940s from a style set by college crew men?

50s

The phrase "two-time loser," previously applied only to criminals, was expanded to include people who failed twice at what?

60s

Who was the only actress to win two Oscars in this decade?

70s

What was the number-one rated TV show for more seasons than any other in the 1970s?

80s

What team destroyed the Washington Redskins in the 1984 Super Bowl?

FUTURE

In 1987, it will be half a century since what event effectively ended travel by airship?

The Decades 70

40s

The term "Mickey Mouse movie" described documentaries intended for what audience?

50s

Who were the two cowboys who dominated the small screen at the dawn of the decade?

60s

Who was the only actor to take home a pair of Oscars in this decade?

70s

What woman shocked the world by marrying Sergei Danyelovich Kauzov in 1978—only to divorce him a year later?

80s

Who wed *Doonesbury* creator Gary Trudeau in 1980?

FUTURE

Name the space base that will be twenty-five years old on July 20, 1994.

Answers: The Decades 69

40s
The crew cut

50s
Marriage

60s
Katharine Hepburn

70s
All in the Family

80s
The Los Angeles Raiders

FUTURE
The explosion of the zeppelin *Hindenburg*

Answers: The Decades 70

40s
Soldiers

50s
The Lone Ranger and Hopalong Cassidy

60s
Peter Ustinov

70s
Christina Onassis

80s
Jane Pauley

FUTURE
Tranquility Base (on the moon)

The Decades 71

40s

How many prime-time series were on ABC in 1947?

50s

What event had seriously diminished Harry Truman's chances of winning a third term, had he elected to run?

60s

Whose book *The Strategy of Peace*, his third, was published in 1960?

70s

Toward the end of the decade, these two banks ran neck-and-neck as the largest in the U.S.

80s

When Ron Reagan, Jr., left the Joffrey Ballet, what did he decide to do for a living?

FUTURE

By 2000, it is predicted that what liquid resource will only be able to meet just over two-thirds of the demand?

The Decades 72

40s

In 1947, Kraft, Gillette, and Esso were the only companies that lent their names to what?

50s

Who was the decade's first Oscar winner for Best Actor?

60s

Name the 1967 movie that marked Spencer Tracy's final film appearance.

70s

As the 1970s ended, what two industrial corporations were the largest in the U.S.—to some degree because the product of one used the product of the other.

80s

By a factor of nearly two to one, what is the world's busiest airport for international flights?

FUTURE

This position will offer more job opportunities through 1990 than any other.

40s
None

50s
The Korean War

60s
John F. Kennedy's

70s
BankAmerica and Citicorp

80s
Become a journalist

FUTURE
Oil

40s
The titles of TV shows

50s
Jose Ferrer, for his performance in *Moulin Rouge*.

60s
Guess Who's Coming to Dinner?

70s
General Motors and Exxon

80s
Heathrow (London)

FUTURE
Secretary

40s
What is the name of the "Fire and Rain" singer born in 1948?

50s
Name the comic strip that made its debut in 1950 and is still going strong—though its creator still thinks the strip has "a terrible name."

60s
In April, 1966, Robert G. Ferry set a record of 2,213 miles for travel in what kind of vehicle?

70s
Who was the presidential candidate of the People's Party in 1972?

80s
What city has the busiest port in the U.S.?

FUTURE
True or false: There will be nearly fifty percent more female than male drivers by 1990.

The Decades 74

40s
Name the future hairdresser who took up arms for Israel in 1948.

50s
Name the future drummer-superstar who dropped out of school in 1954 for a short-lived career in engineering.

60s
In what state is the Lake Pontchartrain Causeway II which, completed in 1969, is the longest bridge in the world?

70s
True or false: General Motors' output of cars during this decade was more than that of American Motors, Ford, and Chrysler combined.

80s
What is the world's busiest airport?

FUTURE
"Telepuppets" is a term coined by Carl Sagan to describe: (a) TV addicts, if viewing patterns continue to increase (b) Landing craft controlled by humans orbiting the planet (c) Personal robots activated by telephone

Answers: The Decades 73

40s
James Taylor

50s
Peanuts

60s
Helicopter

70s
Dr. Benjamin Spock

80s
New York

FUTURE
False. The ratio will be nearly equal.

Answers: The Decades 74

40s
Vidal Sassoon

50s
Ringo Starr

60s
Louisiana

70s
True

80s
O'Hare (Chicago)

FUTURE
b) Landing craft controlled by humans orbiting the planet

The Decades 75

40s

Which president's memorial was completed during World War II?

50s

Name the D. H. Lawrence novel that was at the center of a legal row over the definition of obscenity.

60s

In what 1960 film did actor Tony Perkins play two roles?

70s

Oregan's Trojan was the most powerful one of these in operation during this decade.

80s

What world leader seemed to doze for thirty seconds as he gave a speech in 1984, leading to widespread speculation about his health?

FUTURE

True or false: By 1990, Tokyo will surpass New York as the most expensive city in which to live.

The Decades 76

40s

Born in 1948, what is the more familiar name of the Baron of Renfrew and Lord of the Isles, among other titles?

50s

In what sport did Sweetwater Clifton break the color barrier?

60s

Name the Triple Crown-winning jockey born in 1960.

70s

Name the royal wife of Captain Mark Phillips.

80s

Name the nineteenth-century Italian composer, an unknown opera of whose was discovered in a London basement in May, 1984.

FUTURE

By 2000, the Bureau of the Census projects that what age group will contain more people than any other? (a) Under 10 years old (b) 40–44 (c) Over 65

40s
Thomas Jefferson's

50s
Lady Chatterly's Lover

60s
Psycho

70s
Nuclear power plant

80s
Konstantin Chernenko

FUTURE
False. For years Tokyo already has had that honor.

Answers: The Decades 76

40s
Prince Charles

50s
Basketball

60s
Steve Cauthen

70s
Princess Anne

80s
Gaetano Donizetti

FUTURE
b) 40–44

The Decades 77

40s
What was the coldest temperature ever recorded in North America?
(a) −62°F (b) −38°F (c) −81°F

50s
True or false: Mary Leakey discovered "Nutcracker Man."

60s
Who did Cherylynn La Piere marry in 1964?

70s
True or false: More people were arrested for possession of marijuana than for heroin and cocaine combined.

80s
True or false: The U.S. Supreme Court says that while renting prerecorded videocassettes is legal, taping off the TV is not.

FUTURE
What is the next year that will read the same backward and forward?

The Decades 78

40s
What detective was made famous by Humphrey Bogart in *The Maltese Falcon*?

50s
True or false: James Arness played a space monster in 1951.

60s
When Oroville Dam was completed in 1968, what dam relinquished its crown as the highest in the U.S.?

70s
True or false: While Congress wrestled with legislation throughout the decade, there was a moratorium on capital punishment.

80s
What party was voted into power in El Salvador in May, 1984?

FUTURE
Will the number of Americans living under the poverty level increase or decrease as the twentieth century draws to a close?

40s
c) −81° F

50s
True

60s
Salvatore "Sonny" Bono

70s
True, by a factor of four-to-one

80s
False. It's all legal.

FUTURE
1991

40s
Sam Spade

50s
True. He was the Thing.

60s
Hoover

70s
False

80s
The Christian Democratic Party

FUTURE
Decrease

The Decades 79

40s
Name the luxury liner that rammed and sunk the *Curacao* in 1942.
50s
Name the actress, born in 1959, who was possessed by the devil in the film *The Exorcist*.
60s
What did the Uniform Time Act of 1966 accomplish?
70s
True or false: Chicagoans were more likely to be crime victims than inhabitants of any other city.
80s
The name Farrakhan made headlines in connection with which presidential candidate?
FUTURE
Are Australia and Antarctica drifting together or apart?

The Decades 80

40s
Born in 1942, this actress is famous for her slightly crossed eyes.
50s
President Eisenhower invoked what doctrine to send aid to Jordan in 1957?
60s
Name the four musicals that won Best Picture Oscars during this decade.
70s
For a brief period during the decade, what twin towers were the tallest buildings in the world?
80s
What NOW-backed legislation failed to be ratified?
FUTURE
If trends continue, will more or fewer people die each year in automobile accidents?

40s
The Queen Mary

50s
Linda Blair

60s
It decreed the observance of Daylight Savings Time nationwide

70s
False. New Yorkers stole the prize.

80s
Jesse Jackson

FUTURE
Apart

Answers: The Decades 80

40s
Karen Black

50s
The Truman Doctrine

60s
West Side Story, *My Fair Lady*, *The Sound of Music*, and *Oliver*

70s
The World Trade Center (New York)

80s
The Equal Rights Amendment (ERA)

FUTURE
Fewer

The Decades 81

40s
What sexual study was a 1948 best-seller?

50s
Name the young star who died in 1955, wrecking his Porsche en route to compete in a race.

60s
What film popularized the saying "What we've got here is a failure to communicate"?

70s
What former actress became Assistant Secretary of State in 1976?

80s
What was the claim to fame of the Eastern North Pacific's Agatha, Virgil, and Winifred?

FUTURE
1961 was the last year that read the same right-side-up and upside-down. What will be the next year to hold this dubious honor?

The Decades 82

40s
Name the author who was killed in a car accident in 1940 while racing to a funeral.

50s
What was the famous couple married by Archbishop Cushing at the Auchincloss mansion in 1953?

60s
What surgical operation was first accomplished in South Africa in 1967?

70s
Name the Russian dancer who defected in 1974.

80s
Who married jockey Robyn Smith in 1980?

FUTURE
What is expected to remain the world's most populous city throughout the rest of the decade?

40s
The Kinsey Report

50s
James Dean

60s
Cool Hand Luke

70s
Shirley Temple (Black)

80s
They were all hurricanes

FUTURE
6009

Answers: The Decades 82

40s
Nathanael West

50s
Jacqueline Bouvier and John Kennedy

60s
Human heart transplant

70s
Mikhail Baryshnikov

80s
Fred Astaire

FUTURE
Shanghai

40s

Silent screen star Charlie Chaplin made his talking debut in what film classic?

50s

Which one of these renowned poets did *not* collect a Pulitzer Prize in the 1950s? (a) Carl Sandburg (b) Archibald MacLeish (c) W. H. Auden

60s

From who was Edie Adams widowed in 1962?

70s

In 1978, Nancy Lopez made her professional debut in what sport?

80s

Charles T. Manatt is the chairman of what contentious group?

FUTURE

In what year will the 200th Kentucky Derby be run?

The Decades 84

40s

Lillian Hellman was the basis for what Dashiell Hammett character?

50s

Frank Sinatra won an Oscar for his acting in what 1953 film?

60s

Who preceded Pete Rozelle as NFL commissioner?

70s

Who took the heavyweight title from Muhammad Ali in 1978, one of the biggest upsets in sports history?

80s

How many men were shot in John Hinckley, Jr.'s attempt on the life of President Reagan?

FUTURE

Scientists have suggested that instead of hauling tons of metal into space, we can use what material to build a permanent space station?

Answers: The Decades 83

40s
The Great Dictator

50s
c) W. H. Auden. He won in 1948.

60s
Ernie Kovacs

70s
Golf

80s
The Democratic Party

FUTURE
2074

Answers: The Decades 84

40s
Nora Charles in *The Thin Man*

50s
From Here to Eternity

60s
Bert Bell

70s
Leon Spinks

80s
Four

FUTURE
Lunar rock

The Decades 85

40s

Name the comedians who met Frankenstein in a 1948 box-office monster.

50s

Roy Campanella was the first black to play what position in major league baseball?

60s

What movie starring Spencer Tracy and Fredric March, centered on the Scopes Trial?

70s

Name the entertainer who suffered a brain concussion, fractured jaw, and other breaks in a stage mishap in 1972.

80s

Before his death in 1981, he was the last American five-star general.

FUTURE

What landmark will *The New York Times* achieve on March 14, 1995?

The Decades 86

40s

How many Olympics were canceled in this decade?

50s

Who said, "My heart is a hamloaf" and married Nancy Davis in 1952?

60s

What singer's second big hit was "On The Good Ship Lollipop"?

70s

Flip Wilson made the feisty female Geraldine a household name during the 1970–74 run of his TV series. What was the name of Geraldine's boyfriend?

80s

What actor was with Robert Wagner and Natalie Wood the night the actress drowned?

FUTURE

How many times will Roger Moore have played James Bond when *View to a Kill* is released in 1985?

40s
Abbott and Costello

50s
Catcher

60s
Inherit the Wind

70s
Ann-Margret

80s
Omar N. Bradley

FUTURE
It will publish its 50,000th edition

Answers: The Decades 86

40s
Two. In 1940 and 1944.

50s
Ronald Reagan

60s
Tiny Tim

70s
Killer

80s
Christopher Walken

FUTURE
Seven

The Decades 87

40s
What was Babe Didrikson's sport?

50s
True or false: Stevie Wonder, born in 1950, lost his eyesight two years later after a bout with Scarlet Fever.

60s
After receiving a cartoon of a wolf from a fan, deejay Bob Smith legally changed his name to what?

70s
Whose first book, as an editor for Viking Press, was *In the Russian Style*?

80s
What 1927 Abel Gance film classic was revived in roadshow engagements around the world?

FUTURE
Is the world population creeping up on four or five billion people?

The Decades 88

40s
What city produced three Miss America winners during this decade?

50s
Name the aircraft carrier that sank the destroyer *Hobson* after a 1952 mid-Atlantic collision.

60s
What team won the first Super Bowl?

70s
Name the former SDS leader who wed Jane Fonda in 1973.

80s
What made-for-TV movie portrayed the aftermath of a nuclear war?

FUTURE
What year will mark the 25th anniversary of the first American's trip into space?

40s
Golf

50s
False. He was blind at birth.

60s
Wolfman Jack

70s
Jacqueline Onassis

80s
Napoleon

FUTURE
Five billion

Answers: The Decades 88

40s
Los Angeles

50s
The Wasp

60s
The Green Bay Packers

70s
Tom Hayden

80s
The Day After

FUTURE
1986

The Decades 89

40s
This sex symbol, born in 1940, became a superstar after appearing barely clad in the dinosaur film *One Million Years B.C.*
50s
In the fall of 1957, what genre came from nowhere to dominate prime-time TV programing?
60s
Name the two Yankees who chased Babe Ruth's home-run record in 1961.
70s
Ernest Borgnine and Burt Lancaster both pursued this role in 1972, only to lose it to Marlon Brando.
80s
For what cause did Michael Jackson film TV commercials in the summer of 1984?
FUTURE
What Woody Allen movie predicts a future in which there are robot butlers?

The Decades 90

40s
DuBose Heyward, who died in 1940, wrote the novel that became the basis of what famous Gershwin opera?
50s
Who produced the decade's most popular science-fiction and fantasy films, among them *War of the Worlds*, *Destination Moon*, and *When Worlds Collide*?
60s
Who served as Secretary of State for Presidents Kennedy and Johnson?
70s
Who replaced Thomas Eagleton on the McGovern presidential ticket?
80s
"Karma Chameleon" was a hit for which British band?
FUTURE
What is the goal of the L-5 Society?

40s
Raquel Welch

50s
The Western

60s
Roger Maris and Mickey Mantle

70s
Don Corleone in *The Godfather*

80s
Getting drunk drivers off the road

FUTURE
Sleeper

Answers: The Decades 90

40s
Porgy and Bess

50s
George Pal

60s
Dean Rusk

70s
R. Sargent Shriver

80s
Culture Club

FUTURE
To lobby for the construction of a permanent, inhabited space colony.

The Decades 91

40s

When TV broadcasting began in earnest, there were four networks: NBC, CBS, ABC, and what other?

50s

What Bill Haley single is history's top-selling rock record?

60s

This moviemaker was ruined by the flop of such costly pictures as *Fall of the Roman Empire* and *55 Days at Peking*.

70s

True or false: Nixon got a higher percentage of the popular vote in his *losing* bid for the presidency than when he won in 1968.

80s

How many top-ten singles—a record—were released from Michael Jackson's *Thriller* album?

FUTURE

A tombstone at the Bishop Museum in Honolulu anticipates the death of what due to "wastes [and] numbers"?

The Decades 92

40s

True or false: More Americans fought in World War II than in all other wars combined.

50s

What was Truman's "extension" of the New Deal, which included a higher minimum wage and greater social security benefits?

60s

A film about what lusty, picaresque Henry Fielding hero won the Best Picture Oscar in 1963?

70s

In 1974, what nation's gas group, PEMEX, made news?

80s

Launched with much fanfare in 1983, this Coleco computer proved to be one of the industry's big financial disappointments.

FUTURE

In a 1981 John Carpenter film about 1997, which of our major metropolises has been turned into a maximum security prison?

40s
DuMont

50s
Rock Around the Clock

60s
Samuel Bronston

70s
True

80s
Seven

FUTURE
Humankind

Answers: The Decades 92

40s
False. The other wars combined come to a marginally higher sum.

50s
The Fair Deal

60s
Tom Jones

70s
Mexico's

80s
The Adam

FUTURE
New York (*Escape from New York*)

The Decades 93

40s

In 1946, what republic began an eight-year battle against Communist-led Huk rebels?

50s

Name the three nations of the acronymic Pacific defense pact, ANZUS

60s

True or false: Kennedy was the first President born in the twentieth century.

70s

In 1970, Poland accepted the Oder-Neisse line as a border between itself and what nation?

80s

In 1984, Mattel unloaded this floundering videogame system to a group of investors.

FUTURE

In what year will the U.S. officially relinquish control over the Panama Canal?

The Decades 94

40s

What Brooklyn Dodgers player was the National League's Rookie of the Year in 1947?

50s

In what year did the U.S. finally put an artificial satellite into orbit?

60s

Name the 1963 hit sung by Sister Luc-Gabrielle.

70s

What singer starred in the *Clams on the Half Shell Review*?

80s

True or false: The British fought Argentina on the Malvinas Islands.

FUTURE

Arthur C. Clarke has recently announced a sequel to his successful *2001* and *2010*. In what year is this one to be set?

Answers: The Decades 93

40s
The Philippines

50s
Australia, New Zealand, and the United States

60s
True

70s
West Germany

80s
Intellivision

FUTURE
2000

Answers: The Decades 94

40s
Jackie Robinson

50s
1958

60s
Dominique

70s
Bette Midler

80s
True. They're the Falkland Islands, to the British.

FUTURE
20,001

The Decades 95

40s

What term meaning "a hip or compassionate male" was coined in 1946?

50s

Name the author which *Peyton Place* made famous.

60s

What was Marion Crane doing when she saw Norman Bates for the last time?

70s

Who, born "No Name Maddox," masterminded one of the most sensational crimes of the decade?

80s

In 1984, publisher Rupert Murdoch made an unsuccessful attempt to acquire control of what conglomerate?

FUTURE

In what year do the denizens of the Clavius base find a black monolith buried on the moon?

The Decades 96

40s

What German weapon was nicknamed for the sputtering sound it made?

50s

Malenkov and Bulganin were both leaders of this nation during the 1950s.

60s

Name the tennis star, born in 1962, who became the youngest woman in history to win the U.S. Open.

70s

Who is the host of *Soul Train*, which began airing in 1970 and remains a showcase for up-and-coming black artists?

80s

True or false: The United States boycotted The XX Olympiad to protest Moscow's invasion of Afghanistan.

FUTURE

In what century are the adventures of Buck Rogers set?

Answers: The Decades 95

40s
Daddy-o

50s
Grace Metalious

60s
Taking a shower (in *Psycho*)

70s
Charles Manson

80s
Warner Communications

FUTURE
2001

Answers: The Decades 96

40s
The burp gun

50s
The U.S.S.R.

60s
Tracy Austin

70s
Don Cornelius

80s
False. It was the XXII Olympiad.

FUTURE
The 25th

The Decades 97

40s
The bazooka, an antitank rocket launcher, was named after what?

50s
What star of TV's *The Adventures of Superman*, died of a gunshot wound.

60s
Because of delays in getting production underway on *Cleopatra*, what actor had to be replaced by Richard Burton?

70s
Marvin Gaye and Helen Reddy were two of the principal backers of what famous cookie maker?

80s
During the 1984 Presidential primaries, Walter Mondale frequently invoked the advertising slogan of what restaurant chain?

FUTURE
True or false: The futuristic film *Just Imagine*, made in 1930, was the first science-fiction musical.

The Decades 98

40s
What abbreviation did Lifebuoy soap popularize?

50s
What play won Tennessee Williams a Pulitzer Prize in 1955?

60s
This 1964 release is the most successful film in the history of Walt Disney Productions.

70s
Who took tea with the West German Ambassador in 1977, breaking a longstanding vow never to talk to a German?

80s
True or false: Before his death, Peter Sellers was slated to star in a film entitled *The Pink Panther Has a Baby*.

FUTURE
What London play will celebrate the thirty-fifth year of its unparalleled *continuous* run on November 25, 1987?

40s
A musical instrument of that name, which it resembled

50s
George Reeves

60s
Stephen Boyd

70s
Wally Amos (Famous Amos)

80s
Wendy's ("Where's the Beef")

FUTURE
True

Answers: The Decades 98

40s
B.O.

50s
Cat on a Hot Tin Roof

60s
Mary Poppins

70s
Menachem Begin

80s
True

FUTURE
The Mousetrap

The Decades 99

40s
Name the actor knighted in 1947 by King George VI.

50s
Who fired singer Julius La Rosa from his series during a live broadcast?

60s
What investigative panel counted Gerald Ford and Earl Warren among its members?

70s
Who was divorced from David Harris in 1973?

80s
Who played George Washington in the 1984 TV miniseries?

FUTURE
"Feelies" will be the motion picture entertainment of the future, according to what novel?

The Decades 100

40s
Name the dashing actor whose rape trial made headlines in 1943.

50s
What airborne sporting good was introduced by Wham-O in 1957?

60s
True or false: Lyndon Johnson was the thirty-sixth president of the United States.

70s
In 1977, a six-foot statue of what comic-strip character was unveiled in the park named for his creator, Elzie Crisler Segar.

80s
Impeccable fidelity, no wear and tear, and a complete lack of surface noise helped make what audio systems much in demand?

FUTURE
What California attraction will be fifty years old on July 17, 2005?

Answers: The Decades 99

40s
Laurence Olivier

50s
Arthur Godfrey

60s
The Warren Commission

70s
Joan Baez

80s
Barry Bostwick

FUTURE
Brave New World

Answers: The Decades 100

40s
Errol Flynn

50s
The Frisbee

60s
True

70s
Popeye

80s
Compact Disc Players (CDs)

FUTURE
Disneyland

PART THREE

PEOPLE

People 1

BIBLE
Which gospel writes, "Blessed are the meek: for they shall inherit the earth?"

TV/MOVIE STARS
Who was the movies' first Superman?

POLITICIANS
In 1980, the taking of the hostages in Iran boosted Jimmy Carter's performance in the primaries at the expense of what candidate?

ATHLETES
Who did Muhammad Ali knock out in Kinshasa, Zaire, in 1974?

COUPLES
What couple was united in the Rose Garden of the White House in 1971?

SCIENTISTS AND INVENTORS
What is Dr. Frankenstein's first name?

People 2

BIBLE
What was Esau's profession?

TV/MOVIE STARS
To what comedy team did Shemp Howard belong?

POLITICIANS
In 1984, Senator Lowell Weicker led the opposition to what controversial school issue supported by President Reagan?

ATHLETES
How many career home runs did Babe Ruth have?

COUPLES
He suffered a concussion, she took a spill, and neither did the job they were sent to do. Who are they?

SCIENTISTS AND INVENTORS
Robert H. Goddard is renowned for his work in what upwardly mobile field?

Answers: People 1

BIBLE
Matthew

TV/MOVIE STARS
Kirk Alyn

POLITICIANS
Edward Kennedy

ATHLETES
George Foreman

COUPLES
Tricia Nixon and Ed Cox

SCIENTISTS AND INVENTORS
Victor

Answers: People 2

BIBLE
Hunter

TV/MOVIE STARS
The Three Stooges

POLITICIANS
School prayer

ATHLETES
714

COUPLES
Jack and Jill

SCIENTISTS AND INVENTORS
Rocketry

People 3

BIBLE
To whom did God say, "Be strong and of a good courage"?
TV/MOVIE STARS
Who played Kitty Russell on *Gunsmoke*?
POLITICIANS
After his impeachment, by how many Senate votes was President Andrew Johnson spared the shame of being removed from office?
ATHLETES
What was UCLA basketballer Don Barksdale the first black to be named?
COUPLES
In *Batman*, what is the name of Bruce Wayne's ward?
SCIENTISTS AND INVENTORS
What revealing discovery was made by Wilhelm Roentgen?

People 4

BIBLE
Which of the following was a harlot? (a) Rahab (b) Esther (c) Shiphrah
TV/MOVIE STARS
What is Richard Chamberlain's first name?
POLITICIANS
What was William Henry Harrison the first president to do while in office?
ATHLETES
Ty Cobb was the first baseball player to have 4,000 . . . what?
COUPLES
According to gossip of the time, Cleopatra encouraged Mark Antony's suicide to win favor with whom?
SCIENTISTS AND INVENTORS
Whose work in theoretical physics earned him a Nobel Prize in 1921?

Answers: People 3

BIBLE
David

TV/MOVIE STARS
Amanda Blake

POLITICIANS
One

ATHLETE
All American

COUPLES
Dick Grayson

SCIENTISTS AND INVENTORS
X-rays

Answers: People 4

BIBLE
a) Rahab

TV/MOVIE STARS
George

POLITICIANS
Die

ATHLETES
Safe hits

COUPLES
Octavian (Augustus)

SCIENTISTS AND INVENTORS
Albert Einstein

People 5

BIBLE
Who nursed the baby Moses?

TV/MOVIE STARS
Keith and David are the actor-sons of what Hollywood legend?

POLITICIANS
Hannibal Hamlin was the first vice-president in whose administration?

ATHLETES
Which Dodgers shortstop was the only player to participate in all seven World Series between Brooklyn and the New York Yankees?

COUPLES
Who was husband to Bianca Perez Morena de Macia from 1971–79?

SCIENTISTS AND INVENTORS
Name the Greek that ushered medicine from the realm of superstition.

People 6

BIBLE
What were the names of Zechariah's two staves?

TV/MOVIE STARS
Name the famous author who co-starred in Neil Simon's *Murder By Death*.

POLITICIANS
What New York mayor changed party affiliation and made an unsuccessful bid for the presidency?

ATHLETES
What was Joe Namath's number on the New York Jets?

COUPLES
Whose marriage to Kris Kristofferson was shaken up when Kris performed nude with Sarah Miles in *The Sailor Who Fell From Grace With the Sea*?

SCIENTISTS AND INVENTORS
What medical field did Joseph Lister revolutionize?

Answers: People 5

BIBLE
His natural mother

TV/MOVIE STARS
John Carradine

POLITICIANS
Abraham Lincoln

ATHLETES
Pee Wee Reese

COUPLES
Mick Jagger

SCIENTISTS AND INVENTORS
Hippocrates

Answers: People 6

BIBLE
Beauty and Bands

TV/MOVIE STARS
Truman Capote

POLITICIANS
John Lindsay

ATHLETES
12

COUPLES
Rita Coolidge

SCIENTISTS AND INVENTORS
Surgery

People 7

BIBLE
What was the name of John the Baptist's father?

TV/MOVIE STARS
Name Lloyd Bridges's two actor-sons.

POLITICIANS
True or false: George Washington was not elected by the people of the United States but by Congress.

ATHLETES
Name the American who won the Marathon in the 1972 Munich Olympics.

COUPLES
To whom was Mary Ann Todd married?

SCIENTISTS AND INVENTORS
What future senator was the first Ph.D. on the moon?

People 8

BIBLE
Who, according to Ecclesiastes, know "not any thing"?

TV/MOVIE STARS
What actor, born in Omaha, makes his home in Tahiti?

POLITICIANS
What California governor made an impressive but ultimately unsuccessful run for the presidency in 1976?

ATHLETES
True or false: Leon Spinks's brother Michael won a boxing gold medal in the 1976 Montreal Olympics.

COUPLES
With what superstar did Bill Cosby tour in 1984?

SCIENTISTS AND INVENTORS
Who discovered "arms" around Saturn, which were later determined to be rings?

Answers: People 7

BIBLE
Zacharias

TV/MOVIE STARS
Beau and Jeff

POLITICIANS
False

ATHLETES
Frank Shorter

COUPLES
Abraham Lincoln

SCIENTISTS AND INVENTORS
Harrison H. Schmitt

Answers: People 8

BIBLE
The dead

TV/MOVIE STARS
Marlon Brando

POLITICIANS
Jerry Brown

ATHLETES
True

COUPLES
Sammy Davis, Jr.

SCIENTISTS AND INVENTORS
Galileo

People 9

BIBLE
Who threw Jonah into the water?

TV/MOVIE STARS
Name the *Maude* star who was born Bernice Frankel.

POLITICIANS
Curtis LeMay was the vice-presidential running mate of what candidate?

ATHLETES
What did pitcher W. A. Cummings introduce to baseball in 1866?

COUPLES
Who is Tweety's perennial nemesis?

SCIENTISTS AND INVENTORS
What Cornell University faculty member is also a best-selling popularizer of astronomy?

People 10

BIBLE
Pharaoh gave Solomon the most generous wedding gift in Biblical history. Name it.

TV/MOVIE STARS
What is the surname of the acting brothers who formed a production company called Gluteus Maximus, Inc., in honor of that name.

POLITICIANS
True or false: Abraham Lincoln was elected in 1860 with less than forty percent of the popular vote.

ATHLETES
Bobby Orr helped turn what hockey club into a world class competitor?

COUPLES
What is the last name of *Happy Days'* Howard and Marion?

SCIENTISTS AND INVENTORS
Who devised the Centigrade scale of temperature?

BIBLE
His shipmates

TV/MOVIE STARS
Bea Arthur

POLITICIANS
George Wallace

ATHLETES
The curve ball

COUPLES
Sylvester

SCIENTISTS AND INVENTORS
Carl Sagan

Answers: People 10

BIBLE
The city of Gezer

TV/MOVIE STARS
Bottoms

POLITICIANS
True

ATHLETES
The Boston Bruins

COUPLES
Cunningham

SCIENTISTS AND INVENTORS
Anders Celsius

People 11

BIBLE
Why was it incestuous for Nahor to sleep with Malcah?
TV/MOVIE STARS
Who is Frances Brokaw's controversial daughter?
POLITICIANS
Who was the only Democratic presidential nominee in the 1950s?
ATHLETES
How many perfect scores did Nadia Comaneci tally in the 1976 Olympics?
COUPLES
Name the Curie couple that pioneered research in radioactivity.
SCIENTISTS AND INVENTORS
Which planet was discovered in 1781 by William Herschel?

People 12

BIBLE
Who was Manoah's son, his birth foretold by an angel?
TV/MOVIE STARS
What actor/singer of the 1950s was born Alfred Cocozza?
POLITICIANS
Who was the only U.S. president since Nixon *not* to visit China?
ATHLETES
Name the Pittsburgh Pirate killed in a 1972 plane crash.
COUPLES
True or false: Farrah Fawcett was Lee Majors's first wife.
SCIENTISTS AND INVENTORS
In 1687, what English scientist established the universal laws of motion?

BIBLE
She was Malcah's niece.

TV/MOVIE STARS
Jane Fonda

POLITICIANS
Adlai Stevenson

ATHLETES
Seven

COUPLES
Pierre and Marie

SCIENTISTS AND INVENTORS
Uranus

BIBLE
Samson

TV/MOVIE STARS
Mario Lanza

POLITICIANS
Jimmy Carter

ATHLETES
Roberto Clemente

COUPLES
False. She was his second.

SCIENTISTS AND INVENTORS
Isaac Newton

People 13

BIBLE
What grisly diet do both Isaiah and Ezekiel foretell?

TV/MOVIE STARS
What whining, pratfalling star of *Jumping Jacks* did Groucho Marx dismiss as merely a "puller of faces"?

POLITICIANS
Who was the first American vice-president?

ATHLETES
What former New York Mets player is nicknamed "Mr. Clean"?

COUPLES
Who played the Bride of Frankenstein to Boris Karloff's monster?

SCIENTISTS AND INVENTORS
What English scientist popularized the notion of natural selection among living things?

People 14

BIBLE
True or false: The Pharaoh's chief baker is hanged in Genesis.

TV/MOVIE STARS
Acting opposite Gina Lollobrigida, Anthony Quinn was the third actor to play this deformed character.

POLITICIANS
Who was the first vice-president to die in office?

ATHLETES
Benny Paret died of injuries suffered while boxing what fighter in 1962?

COUPLES
What sports champion is married to John Lloyd?

SCIENTISTS AND INVENTORS
Name the Austrian scientist-monk who formulated the fundamental laws of genetics.

Answers: People 13

BIBLE
Cannibalism

TV/MOVIE STARS
Jerry Lewis

POLITICIANS
John Adams

ATHLETES
Tom Seaver

COUPLES
Elsa Lanchester

SCIENTISTS AND INVENTORS
Charles Darwin

Answers: People 14

BIBLE
True

TV/MOVIE STARS
Quasimodo (The Hunchback of Notre Dame)

POLITICIANS
George Clinton (James Madison's vice-president)

ATHLETES
Emile Griffith

COUPLES
Chris Evert Lloyd

SCIENTISTS AND INVENTORS
Gregor Mendel

People 15

BIBLE
What Amalekite king did Samuel slice to bits?

TV/MOVIE STARS
Just before her untimely death, what buxom actress did *The New York Times* describe as "a weak imitation of Marilyn Monroe"?

POLITICIANS
William E. Miller was the vice-presidential running mate of what Republican candidate?

ATHLETES
Who bought the Dodgers in 1957 and moved them from Brooklyn to Los Angeles?

COUPLES
Name the "poor little rich girl" who was once married to Cary Grant.

SCIENTISTS and INVENTORS
Name the German physicist who lent his name to a "constant."

People 16

BIBLE
To whom did God say, "The end of all flesh is come before me"?

TV/MOVIE STARS
What Japanese star made his English language debut in the 1966 film *Grand Prix*?

POLITICIANS
True or false: Walter Mondale was endorsed by Coretta Scott King in the 1984 presidential primaries.

ATHLETES
Who was the giant slalom gold medalist in the 1968 Olympics?

COUPLES
Who is Underdog's girl friend?

SCIENTISTS AND INVENTORS
What was the 3rd century B.C. astronomer Aristarchus of Samos way ahead of his time in suggesting?

Answers: People 15

BIBLE
Agag

TV/MOVIE STARS
Jayne Mansfield

POLITICIANS
Barry Goldwater

ATHLETES
Walter F. O'Malley

COUPLES
Barbara Hutton

SCIENTISTS AND INVENTORS
Max Planck

Answers: People 16

BIBLE
Noah

TV/MOVIE STARS
Toshiro Mifune

POLITICIANS
True

ATHLETES
Jean-Claude Killy

COUPLES
Sweet Polly Purebread

SCIENTISTS AND INVENTORS
That the earth revolves around the sun

People 17

BIBLE
What lowlife made the empty promise, "Your eyes shall be opened, and ye shall be as gods, knowing good and evil"?

TV/MOVIE STARS
What famous hoofer got to dance opposite Fred Astaire in *Easter Parade*?

POLITICIANS
In 1979, Zulfikar Ali Bhutto was executed. He had been prime minister of what nation?

ATHLETES
Who coached the gold medal-winning U.S. hockey team in the 1980 Olympics?

COUPLES
To what singer is actress Carrie Fisher married?

SCIENTISTS AND INVENTORS
James P. Joule's law of the conservation of energy is more commonly known as what?

People 18

BIBLE
Who spoke for God when chastising David about the way he stole Uriah's wife?

TV/MOVIE STARS
The ads for *Niagara* described both the film and what star as, "a raging torrent of emotion that even nature can't control"?

POLITICIANS
The assassination of what political figure helped to bring on World War I?

ATHLETES
Tom Dempsey kicked the longest field goal in NFL history. How many yards did it travel?

COUPLES
Who is Wilma Deering's boyfriend?

SCIENTISTS AND INVENTORS
What is the better-known name of Claudius Ptolemaeus, the Greek who specialized in celestial mechanics?

BIBLE
The serpent in Eden

TV/MOVIE STARS
Ann Miller

POLITICIANS
Pakistan

ATHLETES
Herb Brooks

COUPLES
Paul Simon

SCIENTISTS AND INVENTORS
The first law of thermodynamics

Answers: People 18

BIBLE
Nathan

TV/MOVIE STARS
Marilyn Monroe

POLITICIANS
Archduke Ferdinand of Austria

ATHLETES
63 yards

COUPLES
Buck Rogers

SCIENTISTS AND INVENTORS
Ptolemy

People 19

BIBLE
What did Joseph's brothers slay in order to cover his coat with blood?   (a) a cow   (b) a goat   (c) a sheep

TV/MOVIE STARS
To which seagoing epic was star Gregory Peck referring when he said, "I still think it all belongs between the covers of a book"?

POLITICIANS
Name the San Francisco mayor shot to death in 1978.

ATHLETES
What is O. J. Simpson's nickname?

COUPLES
Name the rock band in which the four members are two married couples.

SCIENTISTS AND INVENTORS
True or false: The ohm, an electrical unit of resistance, is named for Oliver Henry Mercator.

People 20

BIBLE
Who did God advise to "escape to the mountain, lest thou be consumed"?

TV/MOVIE STARS
What film star, mistakenly thought of as French-born, actually came into the world as Ivo Livi in Milan, Italy?

POLITICIANS
What was the only state carried in 1972 by George McGovern?

ATHLETES
Name the New York Yankees catcher killed when the plane he was piloting crashed in 1979.

COUPLES
What member of the rock group Kiss dated Cher after the breakup of her marriage to Gregg Allman?

SCIENTISTS AND INVENTORS
What is the more familiar name for Polish astronomer Mikolaj Kopernik?

Answers: People 19

BIBLE
b) a goat

TV/MOVIE STARS
Moby Dick

POLITICIANS
George R. Moscone

ATHLETES
"The Juice"

COUPLES
ABBA

SCIENTISTS AND INVENTORS
False. For Georg S. Ohm

Answers: People 20

BIBLE
Lot

TV/MOVIE STARS
Yves Montand

POLITICIANS
Massachusetts

ATHLETES
Thurman Munson

COUPLES
Gene Simmons

SCIENTISTS AND INVENTORS
Copernicus

People 21

BIBLE
What was Abraham's name before God changed it?

TV/MOVIE STARS
Who, known as "America's Sweetheart," died in 1979 at the age of 86?

POLITICIANS
In what country was California congressman Leo Ryan murdered?

ATHLETES
What did Lones Wigger and daughter Deena strive to become in the 1984 Summer Olympics?

COUPLES
Name the husband and wife writers, one of whom wrote *Scruples*, the other *Laurel Canyon*.

SCIENTISTS AND INVENTORS
What hot Benjamin Franklin invention bore his name?

People 22

BIBLE
How many stones did David carry into battle with Goliath?

TV/MOVIE STARS
What Oscar-winning actress miraculously recovered from the three back-to-back strokes she suffered in 1965 while shooting *Seven Women*?

POLITICIANS
To what political superstar is Nancy Maginnes married?

ATHLETES
What did the San Francisco Giants' Bobby Bonds hit his first time at bat in a major league game?   (a) a grand slam   (b) his manager, giving him a concussion   (c) a TV camera

COUPLES
He's tall, and became famous as a dancer. She's skinny, and became famous as a model. Together they starred in the Broadway hit *My One and Only*. Who are they?

SCIENTISTS AND INVENTORS
Name the physiologist who wrote *Conditioned Reflexes* and became famous for his dog.

BIBLE
Abram

TV/MOVIE STARS
Mary Pickford

POLITICIANS
Guyana

ATHLETES
The first-ever father-daughter Olympic teammates

COUPLES
Judith and Steve Krantz

SCIENTISTS AND INVENTORS
The Franklin stove

Answers: People 22

BIBLE
Five

TV/MOVIE STARS
Patricia Neal

POLITICIANS
Henry Kissinger

ATHLETES
a) a grand slam

COUPLES
Tommy Tune and Twiggy

SCIENTISTS AND INVENTORS
Ivan Petrovich Pavlov

People 23

BIBLE
What was the occupation of Potiphar, Joseph's master?

TV/MOVIE STARS
What co-star of the 1968 Best Picture Oscar winner has the same first name as the title of the film?

POLITICIANS
How was the birth of Millard Fillmore, the thirteenth president, unique from those of his predecessors?

ATHLETES
Name the player's association headed by Ed Garvey.

COUPLES
What actress, who is nearing the mid-century mark, married thirty-one-year-old Dr. Robert Levine in 1983?

SCIENTISTS AND INVENTORS
The antiproton was produced and detected by? (a) Neville Chamberlain (b) Wilt Chamberlain (c) Owen Chamberlain

---

People 24

BIBLE
What was Mordecai's blood relation to Esther?

TV/MOVIE STARS
What film and Broadway star once held the dubious title of Miss Burbank?

POLITICIANS
Though he was already out of office, who was the first president to be photographed?

ATHLETES
Mel Ott of the New York Giants was the first player to score how many runs in a major league game?

COUPLES
With what president was Judith Campbell Exner romantically linked?

SCIENTISTS AND INVENTORS
Though Robert W. Bunsen contributed enormously to the science of spectroscopy, he is remembered for what scientific tool?

BIBLE
"An officer of the Pharaoh, captain of the guard"

TV/MOVIE STARS
Oliver Reed

POLITICIANS
He was the first president born in the 19th century.

ATHLETES
National Football League Players Association

COUPLES
Mary Tyler Moore

SCIENTISTS AND INVENTORS
c) Owen Chamberlain

Answers: People 24

BIBLE
They were cousins.

TV/MOVIE STARS
Debbie Reynolds

POLITICIANS
John Quincy Adams

ATHLETES
Six

COUPLES
John F. Kennedy

SCIENTISTS AND INVENTORS
The Bunsen burner

People 25

BIBLE
How long does Mark say the darkness lasted after Jesus' crucifixion?

TV/MOVIE STARS
Whose biographical film, originally announced for Marilyn Monroe and then Lee Remick, was finally made with Carroll Baker?

POLITICIANS
Which one of the first five presidents was not a Virginian?

ATHLETES
True or false: Both Steve Palinkas and his wife Pat played football professionally for the Atlantic Coast League's Orlando Panthers.

COUPLES
Name the actress to whom Burt Reynolds was married.

SCIENTISTS AND INVENTORS
J. Robert Oppenheimer subsequently had second thoughts about what device, whose development he oversaw?

People 26

BIBLE
After Jonah spent some time under water, where did God send him?

TV/MOVIE STARS
Name the only Egyptian actor to become an international film star.

POLITICIANS
Name the town and state in which John F. Kennedy was born.

ATHLETES
Who was the oldest player in the history of major league baseball?

COUPLES
What was the name of Miss Lillian Carter's husband?

SCIENTISTS AND INVENTORS
Father of the hydrogen bomb, Edward Teller, inspired the creation of which famous movie character?

Answers: People 25

BIBLE
Three hours

TV/MOVIE STARS
Jean Harlow's

POLITICIANS
Massachusetts's John Adams

ATHLETES
True. Pat saw action in only one game.

COUPLES
Judy Carne

SCIENTISTS AND INVENTORS
The atom bomb

Answers: People 26

BIBLE
Ninevah

TV/MOVIE STARS
Omar Sharif

POLITICIANS
Brookline, MA

ATHLETES
Satchel Paige, who pitched his last game at age fifty-nine

COUPLES
Earl

SCIENTISTS AND INVENTORS
Dr. Strangelove

People 27

BIBLE
Of what was Nebuchadnezzar king?

TV/MOVIE STARS
Who tied with Barbra Streisand for the Best Actress Oscar in 1968?

POLITICIANS
True or false: The parents of former general Dwight Eisenhower belonged to a religious sect that was expressly opposed to war and violence.

ATHLETES
Willie O'Ree was the first black to play in what league professionally?

COUPLES
Karen and Richard Carpenter were   (a) husband and wife   (b) brother and sister   (c) unrelated, using those names only for the stage

SCIENTISTS AND INVENTORS
Whitcomb Judson locked up a patent for what invention?

People 28

BIBLE
Was Salome present at the crucifixion?

TV/MOVIE STARS
What musical superstar played a saloon pianist in *South Sea Sinner*?

POLITICIANS
What political office did Franklin Roosevelt hold before winning the presidency?

ATHLETES
Who fought and fatally kayoed boxer Duk Koo-Kim in 1982?

COUPLES
Name the *Star Trek* star who appeared in a margarine commercial with his wife.

SCIENTISTS AND INVENTORS
For what device, operable by one, two, or ten fingers, was Henry Mills awarded a patent in 1714?

Answers: People 27

BIBLE
Babylon

TV/MOVIE STARS
Katharine Hepburn

POLITICIANS
True

ATHLETES
The National Hockey League

COUPLES
b) brother and sister

SCIENTISTS AND INVENTORS
The zipper

Answers: People 28

BIBLE
Yes

TV/MOVIE STARS
Liberace

POLITICIANS
Governor of New York

ATHLETES
Ray "Boom-Boom" Mancini

COUPLES
William Shatner

SCIENTISTS AND INVENTORS
The typewriter

People 29

BIBLE
To whom did Jesus say, "Except a man be born again, he cannot see the kingdom of God"?

TV/MOVIE STARS
Who uttered *To Have and Have Not*'s immortal line, "You know how to whistle, don't you? You just put your lips together—and blow."

POLITICIANS
What president was assassinated after being in office only four months?

ATHLETES
Lou Gehrig, a baseball great, was nonetheless the first to do what in an All-Star game?   (a) commit an error   (b) strike out   (c) hit into a double play

COUPLES
What entertainer's ex-wife did Gary Morton marry?

SCIENTISTS AND INVENTORS
The 17th century scientist Robert Hooke was the first to use what newly invented ocular instrument extensively?

People 30

BIBLE
True or false: Jochebed was both mother and great aunt to Moses?

TV/MOVIE STARS
Name the actress who has had children by both Roger Vadim and Marcello Mastroianni—neither of whom were her husband.

POLITICIANS
How were Presidents Theodore and Franklin Roosevelt related?

ATHLETES
Which one of these is not a football hall-of-famer?   (a) Sam Huff   (b) Roman Gabriel   (c) Dick Butkus

COUPLES
Husband and wife Melvin Kaminsky and Annemarie Italiano are better known by what names?

SCIENTISTS AND INVENTORS
In 1935, Carl Magee invented what coin-gobbling timekeeper?

BIBLE
Nicodemus

TV/MOVIE STARS
Lauren Bacall

POLITICIANS
James Garfield

ATHLETES
a) commit an error

COUPLES
Desi Arnaz's

SCIENTISTS AND INVENTORS
The microscope

Answers: People 30

BIBLE
True

TV/MOVIE STARS
Catherine Deneuve

POLITICIANS
They were fifth cousins

ATHLETES
b) Roman Gabriel

COUPLES
Mel Brooks and Anne Bancroft

SCIENTISTS AND INVENTORS
The parking meter

People 31

BIBLE
What was done for the first time in the river Jordan?

TV/MOVIE STARS
Which of these sons of famous actors is *not* a screenwriter?
(a) Fraser Heston   (b) William Lancaster   (c) Bela Lugosi, Jr.

POLITICIANS
Before Jimmy Carter, who was the last president to be elected from a southern state?

ATHLETES
Tommy Milton was the first man to win what race twice?

COUPLES
Who is the husband of the former Thelma "Pat" Ryan?

SCIENTISTS AND INVENTORS
True or false: One of Thomas Edison's lesser-known inventions was the key-cutting machine.

People 32

BIBLE
Who was the brains behind the defeat of the Canaanite army by the Israelites?   (a) Deborah   (b) Joshua   (c) David

TV/MOVIE STARS
What famous comedian played Mork's son on *Mork and Mindy*?

POLITICIANS
What is the correct form of address for a foreign ambassador?

ATHLETES
Who scored the most (100) points ever tallied by a professional basketball player?

COUPLES
Who sued Lee Marvin in a famous "palimony" suit?

SCIENTISTS AND INVENTORS
In the closing years of the 19th century, Jesse Reno and Charles Seeberger designed what uplifting device?

Answers: People 31

BIBLE
John performed a baptism

TV/MOVIE STARS
c) Bela Lugosi, Jr.

POLITICIANS
Zachary Taylor

ATHLETES
The Indianapolis 500

COUPLES
Richard Nixon

SCIENTISTS AND INVENTORS
False

Answers: People 32

BIBLE
a) Deborah

TV/MOVIE STARS
Jonathan Winters

POLITICIANS
His/Her Excellency

ATHLETES
Wilt Chamberlain

COUPLES
Michelle Triola (Marvin)

SCIENTISTS AND INVENTORS
The escalator

People 33

BIBLE
In his Sermon on the Mount, what does Jesus say cannot be hid?

TV/MOVIE STARS
Who played Bill Bixby's green-skinned alter ego on TV?

POLITICIANS
Who was the first President not to complete his term in office?
(a) Andrew Jackson (b) William H. Harrison (c) Abraham Lincoln

ATHLETES
Name the Olympic star who was also the first professional football commissioner.

COUPLES
In 1980, this comedian split from Patti Palmer, his wife of thirty-six years.

SCIENTISTS AND INVENTORS
What did Jean-Baptiste Jolly invent after accidentally spilling paraffin on a tablecloth?

People 34

BIBLE
Who nearly perished by dropping from a window after falling asleep during one of Paul's sermons?

TV/MOVIE STARS
Before she became famous, what TV star provided the voice for Ms. Flintstone on the *Pebbles and Bamm Bamm Show*?

POLITICIANS
Which one of these candidates did the Republicans *not* serve up as a sacrificial lamb against Franklin Roosevelt? (a) Wendell Wilkie (b) Herbert Hoover (c) Eugene V. Debs

ATHLETES
What position did baseball legend Cy Young play?

COUPLES
As Mrs. John Y. Brown, Phyllis George became the first lady of what state?

SCIENTISTS AND INVENTORS
Name the engineering tool invented by English clergyman William Oughtred.

Answers: People 33

BIBLE
A city set on a hill

TV/MOVIE STARS
Lou Ferrigno

POLITICIANS
b) William H. Harrison

ATHLETES
Jim Thorpe

COUPLES
Jerry Lewis

SCIENTISTS AND INVENTORS
Dry cleaning

Answers: People 34

BIBLE
Eutychus

TV/MOVIE STARS
Sally Struthers

POLITICIANS
c) Eugene V. Debs

ATHLETES
Pitcher

COUPLES
Kentucky

SCIENTISTS AND INVENTORS
The slide rule

People 35

BIBLE
What was the name of David's rebellious son?

TV/MOVIE STARS
Who is the mother of Jason Gould?

POLITICIANS
Whom did Margaret Thatcher replace as Britain's prime minister?

ATHLETES
What boxer handed Muhammad Ali his first professional loss?

COUPLES
She didn't want any part of him, but John Hinckley was allegedly trying to get this actress's attention when he shot President Reagan.

SCIENTISTS AND INVENTORS
In 1827, John Walker struck more than a blow for progress with what invention?

People 36

BIBLE
Who is the first figure to become drunk in the Bible?

TV/MOVIE STARS
What TV star wrote volumes of poetry entitled *Touch Me* and *Touch Me Again*?

POLITICIANS
Who was elected French President upon the death of Georges Pompidou?

ATHLETES
Who was the first foreign player to win America's Masters Tournament?

COUPLES
Name the actor to whom Shirlee Adams was married at the time of his death.

SCIENTISTS AND INVENTORS
James Ritty invented the "Dial Machine" in 1879 to keep employees honest, then sold the patent for $1,000. What commercial blockbuster had he virtually given away?

BIBLE
Absalom

TV/MOVIE STARS
Barbra Streisand

POLITICIANS
James Callaghan

ATHLETES
Joe Frazier

COUPLES
Jodie Foster

SCIENTISTS AND INVENTORS
The friction match

Answers: People 35

BIBLE
Noah, after planting the first vineyard following the flood

TV/MOVIE STARS
Suzanne Somers

POLITICIANS
Giscard Valéry d'Estaing

ATHLETES
Gary Player

COUPLES
Henry Fonda

SCIENTISTS AND INVENTORS
The cash register

People 37

BIBLE
How many years is Methuselah alleged to have lived?

TV/MOVIE STARS
What is the name of Brooke Shields's mother?

POLITICIANS
Who was mayor of Cleveland when, in 1978, the city defaulted and avoided bankruptcy with a fifty-percent tax increase?

ATHLETES
Baseball star Bob Gibson also played basketball for what non-NBA pro team?

COUPLES
What actress married musicmakers Frank Sinatra and Andre Previn, only to find that relations with both men were anything but harmonious?

SCIENTISTS AND INVENTORS
In 1835, W. H. Fox Talbot took a picture of a latticed window with a new photographic process, creating the first what?

People 38

BIBLE
Which of these is not true about Solomon? (a) he had one thousand wives and concubines (b) he knew three thousand proverbs (c) he spent thirteen years building the Temple

TV/MOVIE STARS
Mr. Savalas's first name, Telly, is short for what?

POLITICIANS
Dixy Lee Ray was governor of what state?

ATHLETES
Who is the only college player to win the Heisman Trophy twice?

COUPLES
Who is Dudley Do-Right's inamorata?

SCIENTISTS AND INVENTORS
Alessandro Volta designed the first crude form of this in 1800, and its output was named in his honor.

Answers: People 37

BIBLE
969 years

TV/MOVIE STARS
Teri Shields

POLITICIANS
Dennis J. Kucinich

ATHLETES
The Harlem Globetrotters

COUPLES
Mia Farrow

SCIENTISTS AND INVENTORS
Photographic negative

Answers: People 38

BIBLE
c) he spent thirteen years building the Temple. Solomon spent 13 years building his palace, only 7 on the Temple.

TV/MOVIE STARS
Aristoteles

POLITICIANS
Washington

ATHLETES
Archie Griffin

COUPLES
Sweet Nell

SCIENTISTS AND INVENTORS
The battery

People 39

BIBLE
His name, in Hebrew, means "fish," and he was Joshua's father.

TV/MOVIE STARS
Which of these sons starred in a sequel to one of his father's classic films: (a) Edward Albert   (b) Chris Lemmon   (c) Sean Flynn

POLITICIANS
Who beat Richard Nixon in the 1962 race for the governorship of California?

ATHLETES
Who is the only football player to have won the Super Bowl's "Most Valuable Player" citation twice?

COUPLES
To whom have both Debbie Reynolds and Elizabeth Taylor been married?

SCIENTISTS AND INVENTORS
What was the last name of the German physicist who created the first mercury thermometer?

People 40

BIBLE
How many Israelites did Moses order to be massacred because of their role in the building of the golden calf?   (a) 30   (b) 300   (c) 3000

TV/MOVIE STARS
Name the *Dynasty* actress who rose to early popularity in her role as Audra Barkley on *The Big Valley*.

POLITICIANS
What does the *R* stand for in Gerald R. Ford?

ATHLETES
Who was the first player to participate in more than fifty World Series games?

COUPLES
What actor is married to the heiress of both the Post cereal and EF Hutton fortunes?

SCIENTISTS AND INVENTORS
Who is considered to be the father of both the helicopter and central heating?

Answers: People 39

BIBLE
Nun

TV/MOVIE STARS
c) Sean Flynn. He starred in *The Son of Captain Blood*.

POLITICIANS
Edmund (Pat) Brown

ATHLETES
Bart Starr

COUPLES
Eddie Fisher

SCIENTISTS AND INVENTORS
Fahrenheit

Answers: People 40

BIBLE
c) 30

TV/MOVIE STARS
Linda Evans

POLITICIANS
Rudolph

ATHLETES
Joe DiMaggio

COUPLES
Cliff Robertson (Dina Merrill is his wife)

SCIENTISTS AND INVENTORS
Leonardo da Vinci

People 41

BIBLE
What does Matthew say the poor man did with his one coin for fear of losing it?   (a) he ate it   (b) he buried it   (c) he spent it

TV/MOVIE STARS
Who played James Bond on TV?

POLITICIANS
The "Dixiecrats" nominated who for president in 1948, objecting to the civil rights aspect of the Democratic platform?

ATHLETES
For what team was Hank Aaron playing when he retired?

COUPLES
To what actor was Carole Lombard married when she met future husband Clark Gable?

SCIENTISTS AND INVENTORS
What was the first name of astronomer Halley?

People 42

BIBLE
From what mountain did Moses see all of the promised land?

TV/MOVIE STARS
Name the young girl who was the star of *Firestarter*.

POLITICIANS
What does the *E* stand for in Governor Thomas E. Dewey?

ATHLETES
True or false: The New York Knicks were the first basketball team to sign a female player.

COUPLES
She has been married to Conrad Hilton and George Sanders, among five others. Who is she?

SCIENTISTS AND INVENTORS
What three-camera movie system was designed by inventor Fred Waller?

Answers: People 41

BIBLE
b) he buried it

TV/MOVIE STARS
Barry Nelson

POLITICIANS
Strom Thurmond

ATHLETES
Milwaukee Brewers

COUPLES
William Powell

SCIENTISTS AND INVENTORS
Edmund

Answers: People 42

BIBLE
Mount Nebo

TV/MOVIE STARS
Drew Barrymore

POLITICIANS
Edmund

ATHLETES
False. It was the Indiana Pacers.

COUPLES
Zsa Zsa Gabor

SCIENTISTS AND INVENTORS
Cinerama

People 43

BIBLE
How old was Abraham's wife Sarah when she died?   (a) 127   (b) 77   (c) 27

TV/MOVIE STARS
What diminutive actor provided the voice for one of the first animated cartoon characters, Oswald the Rabbit?

POLITICIANS
What was the political party of George Washington?

ATHLETES
In 1979, New York Islanders Bill Smith was the first goalie in professional hockey history to do what?

COUPLES
Name the film star and sexual athlete who seduced Eva "Evita" Peron and had to flee Argentina after Peron's President-husband found out.

SCIENTISTS AND INVENTORS
Who was the printer that devised a way of printing with movable type?

People 44

BIBLE
How many Philistines died when Samson brought down the house?   (a) 3,000   (b) 6,000   (c) 9,000

TV/MOVIE STARS
Name the only actor to have played President Andrew Jackson in two different films.

POLITICIANS
What popular purchase, made by Thomas Jefferson, clinched his reelection in 1804?

ATHLETES
Name the first horse to win the Triple Crown.

COUPLES
Provide the full name of the character who married Ted Baxter on *The Mary Tyler Moore Show*.

SCIENTISTS AND INVENTORS
Who invented the phonograph?

BIBLE
a) 127

TV/MOVIE STARS
Mickey Rooney

POLITICIANS
Federalist

ATHLETES
Score a goal

COUPLES
Errol Flynn

SCIENTISTS AND INVENTORS
Johannes Gutenberg

BIBLE
6) 6,000. 3000 on the roof, 3000 in the grandstands.

TV/MOVIE STARS
Charlton Heston (*The President's Lady* and *The Buccaneer*)

POLITICIANS
The Louisiana Purchase

ATHLETES
Sir Barton

COUPLES
Georgette Franklin

SCIENTISTS AND INVENTORS
Thomas Edison

People 45

BIBLE
What kind of weapon did the cherubim wield to guard the entrance to Eden?

TV/MOVIE STARS
What explosive TV star, STP spokesperson, and former Our Gang child star was born Michael Gubitosi?

POLITICIANS
The late Frank Church was senator from what state?

ATHLETES
Who was the first black to hold the heavyweight boxing title?

COUPLES
Who was R2-D2's mechanical sidekick?

SCIENTISTS AND INVENTORS
Name the engineer who built the first steamboat.

People 46

BIBLE
True or false: The Bible tells us that the burning bush through which God talked to Moses was a blackberry bush.

TV/MOVIE STARS
What was the first name of Gabe Kaplan's character on *Welcome Back, Kotter*?

POLITICIANS
True or false: Adlai Stevenson, grandfather of the Democratic presidential nominee, was vice-president of the United States.

ATHLETES
Who was the only athlete to have his own animated cartoon series?

COUPLES
What were the last names of Bonnie and Clyde?

SCIENTISTS AND INVENTORS
Who built an observatory—which bears his name—primarily to study what he thought were canals on Mars?

Answers: People 45

BIBLE
A flaming sword

TV/MOVIE STARS
Robert Blake

POLITICIANS
Idaho

ATHLETES
Jack Johnson

COUPLES
C-3PO

SCIENTISTS AND INVENTORS
Robert Fulton

Answers: People 46

BIBLE
False. The Bible says nothing on the matter.

TV/MOVIE STARS
Gabe

POLITICIANS
True

ATHLETES
Muhammad Ali

COUPLES
(Bonnie) Parker and (Clyde) Barrow

SCIENTISTS AND INVENTORS
Percival Lowell

People 47

BIBLE
How did Paul escape from Damascus?

TV/MOVIE STARS
Name the would-be evening news anchor who jumped from CBS to NBC when Dan Rather was named to replace Walter Cronkite.

POLITICIANS
What former two-term president, disapproving of protegé William H. Taft's first term, ran against Taft, split the Republican party, and thus handed the Oval office to Woodrow Wilson?

ATHLETES
Who was Russia's gymnastic star in the 1972 Olympics?

COUPLES
Anne of the Thousand Days is a film about the troubled romance of which two historical figures?

SCIENTISTS AND INVENTORS
Whose book, *Dialogues on the Two Chief World Systems*, saw its author hauled before the Inquisition?

People 48

BIBLE
Who battled King Og at Edrei?

TV/MOVIE STARS
Who played a nurse on *The Rookies* before making detective on *Charlie's Angels*?

POLITICIANS
True or false: Just under one million votes separated John Kennedy and Richard Nixon in the 1960 Presidential race.

ATHLETES
Who was the first tennis player to win a "grand slam"—the U.S. Open, Wimbledon, and championships in Australia and France?

COUPLES
What furry fellow fell for Ann Darrow in a 1933 film?

SCIENTISTS AND INVENTORS
Who commanded the first shuttle flight into space?

BIBLE
He was lowered over the city walls in a basket.

TV/MOVIE STARS
Roger Mudd

POLITICIANS
Theodore Roosevelt

ATHLETES
Olga Korbut

COUPLES
Anne Boleyn and King Henry VIII

SCIENTISTS AND INVENTORS
Galileo

Answers: People 48

BIBLE
Moses

TV/MOVIE STARS
Kate Jackson

POLITICIANS
False. Just over 100,000 votes separated the candidates.

ATHLETES
Don Budge

COUPLES
King Kong

SCIENTISTS AND INVENTORS
John Young

People 49

BIBLE
To top off his other problems, who had a vision of sea serpents?

TV/MOVIE STARS
Name the Saturday morning cartoon character whose voice was provided by Michael Jackson.

POLITICIANS
Which two of these candidates won the presidency, though they earned less of the popular vote than their rivals? (a) Rutherford B. Hayes (b) Harry Truman (c) Benjamin Harrison

ATHLETES
Who was the first athlete in history to win seven gold medals in one Olympics?

COUPLES
Who teamed with Jennifer Warnes to sing the Oscar-winning song "Up Where We Belong" from *An Officer and a Gentleman*?

SCIENTISTS AND INVENTORS
What was the first name of engineer and aerodynamic researcher Eiffel, designer of the Eiffel Tower?

People 50

BIBLE
Who was the second most-famous son of Amram and Jochebed?

TV/MOVIE STARS
What is the last name of John Clark, a legendary film star's only child?

POLITICIANS
Of what state was the late Henry M. "Scoop" Jackson senator?

ATHLETES
Name the French skiier who won three gold medals at the 1968 Winter Olympics in Grenoble, France.

COUPLES
What are the first names of the late, great writing Durants?

SCIENTISTS AND INVENTORS
Who was the second American to orbit the earth?

Answers: People 49

BIBLE
Job

TV/MOVIE STARS
Michael Jackson (on *The Jackson Five* animated series)

POLITICIANS
a) Rutherford B. Hayes and c) Benjamin Harrison

ATHLETES
Mark Spitz

COUPLES
Joe Cocker

SCIENTISTS AND INVENTORS
Alexandre

Answers: People 50

BIBLE
Aaron

TV/MOVIE STARS
Gable

POLITICIANS
Washington

ATHLETES
Jean-Claude Killy

COUPLES
Will and Ariel

SCIENTISTS AND INVENTORS
M. Scott Carpenter

People 51

BIBLE
True or false: David placed the head of a bear behind his throne.
TV/MOVIE STARS
Name the film star who was born Natasha Gurdin.
POLITICIANS
Who was Jimmy Carter's second secretary of state?
ATHLETES
What was the greatest number of home runs Henry Aaron hit in a single season?
COUPLES
Who did David McCallum lose to Charles Bronson?
SCIENTISTS AND INVENTORS
What did Stephen Wozniak and Steven Jobs invent?

People 52

BIBLE
How did Eleazar the Maccabean die, leaving more than his family crushed?
TV/MOVIE STARS
Who played the lead role in *W. C. Fields and Me*?
POLITICIANS
Name the colonial activist who led the Boston Tea Party.
ATHLETES
True or false: Muhammad Ali once received $6.5 million for a single fight.
COUPLES
True or false: Paul Newman is Joanne Woodward's first husband.
SCIENTISTS AND INVENTORS
Name the popular science author who is also head of NASA's Goddard Institute for Space Studies.

Answers: People 51

BIBLE
False

TV/MOVIE STARS
Natalie Wood

POLITICIANS
Ed Muskie

ATHLETES
47 (1971)

COUPLES
Wife Jill Ireland

SCIENTISTS AND INVENTORS
The Apple Computer

Answers: People 52

BIBLE
He was flattened by an elephant.

TV/MOVIE STARS
Rod Steiger

POLITICIANS
Sam Adams

ATHLETES
True. It was against Ken Norton in 1976.

COUPLES
True

SCIENTISTS AND INVENTORS
Robert Jastrow

People 53

BIBLE
What was Abel's profession?

TV/MOVIE STARS
Early in his career, what superstar actor appeared in the porn film *A Party at Kitty and Stud's,* and on the stage in the nude musical *Score*?

POLITICIANS
Where did Jimmy Carter fly to meet the released American hostages?

ATHLETES
True or false: Nolan Ryan, the fastest pitcher in baseball history, threw at speeds in excess of 150 mph.

COUPLES
Name the ex-wife of Andy Williams who stood trial for murder.

SCIENTISTS AND INVENTORS
Alexander Graham Bell may have invented the telephone, but what did the more mercenary William Gray invent?

People 54

BIBLE
Under what kind of tree were Saul and his sons buried?

TV/MOVIE STARS
Name the actor who walked off the set of the movie *10*, giving Dudley Moore the role of a lifetime.

POLITICIANS
What infamous Roman political figure was the son of Agrippina the Younger?

ATHLETES
Governor-General Lord Stanley was the first to present what sports award?

COUPLES
What world leader was married to the former Margaret Sinclair?

SCIENTISTS AND INVENTORS
Which American inventor gave a twist to the presidency by inventing the swivel chair?

Answers: People 53

BIBLE
Shepherd

TV/MOVIE STARS
Sylvester Stallone

POLITICIANS
Wiesbaden, West Germany

ATHLETES
False. His top speed was 100.9 mph.

COUPLES
Claudine Longet

SCIENTISTS AND INVENTORS
The pay phone

Answers: People 54

BIBLE
An oak

TV/MOVIE STARS
George Segal

POLITICIANS
Nero

ATHLETES
Hockey's Stanley Cup

COUPLES
Pierre Trudeau

SCIENTISTS AND INVENTORS
Thomas Jefferson

People 55

BIBLE
Who was accused of strangling her seven husbands?

TV/MOVIE STARS
What does the *C* stand for in George C. Scott?

POLITICIANS
Who was the famous British administrator and general killed by Moslems at Khartoum?

ATHLETES
What unfortunate record is held by quarterback Roman Gabriel?   (a) most career fumbles   (b) most sacks   (c) most yardage lost in a playoff

COUPLES
Who was the only one of her first six husbands from whom Elizabeth Taylor was widowed and not divorced?

SCIENTISTS AND INVENTORS
In 1897, Dr. William Morton fired a bullet into a corpse and was the first to use what device on the human body?

People 56

BIBLE
When Tamar gave birth to twins, what did the midwife do to keep track of the firstborn?

TV/MOVIE STARS
John Ritter is the son of what musical superstar?

POLITICIANS
What nationality was Che Guevara?   (a) Cuban   (b) Argentinian   (c) Bolivian

ATHLETES
What ex-basketball superstar is now a New Jersey senator?

COUPLES
Who is the wife of Edgar Rosenberg?

SCIENTISTS AND INVENTORS
Joseph Baermann Strauss was the chief engineer of what bridge, completed in 1937, and the first with piers sunk in the open sea?

BIBLE
Sarah

TV/MOVIE STARS
Campbell

POLITICIANS
Charles "Chinese" Gordon (Gordon of Khartoum)

ATHLETES
a) most career fumbles

COUPLES
Michael Todd

SCIENTISTS AND INVENTORS
An X-ray machine

Answers: People 56

BIBLE
She tied a scarlet thread around its wrist.

TV/MOVIE STARS
Tex Ritter

POLITICIANS
b) Argentinian

ATHLETES
Bill Bradley

COUPLES
Joan Rivers

SCIENTISTS AND INVENTORS
The Golden Gate Bridge

People 57

BIBLE
Why weren't the evil Hivites up for the battle against Jacob's sons?

TV/MOVIE STARS
Whose last film was *The Killers* in 1964?

POLITICIANS
Was it Alexander Hamilton or Aaron Burr who died in their famous duel?

ATHLETES
What is Yogi Berra's real name?

COUPLES
Who was in love with Aldonza?

SCIENTISTS AND INVENTORS
In what field of science did Margaret Mead work?

People 58

BIBLE
What is the most common name in the Bible?

TV/MOVIE STARS
Name the film and TV comic who was arrested in 1978 for emptying a .357 magnum into a car parked in his driveway.

POLITICIANS
True or false: Franklin and Eleanor Roosevelt were cousins.

ATHLETES
At four seconds, Bobby Unser did what faster than any other driver in racing history?

COUPLES
Who did Donald Duck and Jay Gatsby love?

SCIENTISTS AND INVENTORS
What element did Joseph Priestley discover?

Answers: People 57

BIBLE
They were weak from having recently been circumcised.

TV/MOVIE STARS
Ronald Reagan's.

POLITICIANS
Hamilton, though the career of the vice-president was ruined

ATHLETES
Lawrence P. Berra

COUPLES
Don Quixote

SCIENTISTS AND INVENTORS
Anthropology

Answers: People 58

BIBLE
Zechariah

TV/MOVIE STARS
Richard Pryor

POLITICIANS
True

ATHLETES
Made a pit stop. He got gas and was off.

COUPLES
Daisy

SCIENTISTS AND INVENTORS
Oxygen

People 59

BIBLE
With what was Abraham prepared to slay his son?

TV/MOVIE STARS
Name the late star of *Black Sunday* and *The Deep*, who also wrote the classic play *The Man in the Glass Booth*.

POLITICIANS
What president married Elizabeth Virginia Wallace in Independence, MO?

ATHLETES
Name the field-goal kicker who had only one hand and half of his kicking foot?

COUPLES
Sondra Locke is the girl friend and regular co-star of what movie superstar?

SCIENTISTS AND INVENTORS
For his research in what field is Lord Kelvin best known?

People 60

BIBLE
Of what crime was Michal, daughter of King Saul, guilty?

TV/MOVIE STARS
Name the movie star who was featured on the cover of *Life* more often than any of her peers.

POLITICIANS
Abe Beame was mayor of what city?

ATHLETES
What is the real name of ex-baseball star Whitey Ford?

COUPLES
Whom did secretary Marilyn Barnett sue for palimony?

SCIENTISTS AND INVENTORS
In what field did Tycho Brahe and Johannes Kepler work?

Answers: People 59

BIBLE
A knife

TV/MOVIE STARS
Robert Shaw

POLITICIANS
Harry Truman

ATHLETES
Tom Dempsey

COUPLES
Clint Eastwood

SCIENTISTS AND INVENTORS
Thermometry

Answers: People 60

BIBLE
Bigamy

TV/MOVIE STARS
Elizabeth Taylor

POLITICIANS
New York

ATHLETES
Edward C. Ford

COUPLES
Billie Jean King

SCIENTISTS AND INVENTORS
Astronomy

People 61

BIBLE
What gift did God bestow upon the earth in honor of Noah and those who had survived the flood?

TV/MOVIE STARS
Name the rock star who made his screen debut in the second remake of *The Jazz Singer*.

POLITICIANS
Who headed the FBI prior to J. Edgar Hoover?

ATHLETES
Who scored the winning overtime points in the classic 1958 title match between the Baltimore Colts and the New York Giants?

COUPLES
Who was the lover of the Duke of Buckingham in *The Three Musketeers*?

SCIENTISTS AND INVENTORS
Dr. Vladimir Zworykin, inventor of the iconoscope, is considered the father of what?

People 62

BIBLE
What article of clothing was Moses made to doff at the burning bush?

TV/MOVIE STARS
True or false: Alex Haley played himself on the sequel to *Roots*.

POLITICIANS
As leader of the Continental Congress, who is often referred to as having been the first President of the United States?

ATHLETES
What was Red Grange's real first name?

COUPLES
Who drowns herself after she is spurned and abused by Hamlet?

SCIENTISTS AND INVENTORS
What piece of sports equipment was invented by Frederick Winthrop Thayer in 1878?

BIBLE
The rainbow

TV/MOVIE STARS
Neil Diamond

POLITICIANS
William J. Burns

ATHLETES
Alan Ameche

COUPLES
Anne of Austria

SCIENTISTS AND INVENTORS
Television

Answers: People 62

BIBLE
His shoes

TV/MOVIE STARS
False. James Earl Jones played Haley.

POLITICIANS
John Hancock

ATHLETES
Harold

COUPLES
Ophelia

SCIENTISTS AND INVENTORS
The baseball catcher's mask

People 63

BIBLE
What part of his body does the pharaoh break in the Book of Ezekiel?

TV/MOVIE STARS
With *Shogun* and *The Thorn Birds* under his belt, what actor is considered the "King of the Mini-series"?

POLITICIANS
Name the cabinet post that was first filled by Samuel Osgood.

ATHLETES
What baseball team was Roger Hornsby managing when they won their first pennant in 1926?

COUPLES
What were the first names of the ill-fated lovers in *West Side Story*?

SCIENTISTS AND INVENTORS
Isaac Merritt Singer is noted for his patents on what piece of equipment?

People 64

BIBLE
Which of King Saul's belongings was displayed in the Philistine temple of Dagon?

TV/MOVIE STARS
Born Maurice Micklewhite, he is the world's most famous Cockney actor. What name is he known by?

POLITICIANS
Who was Gerald Ford's secretary of state?

ATHLETES
Name the player who, in 1984, was to reach the pinnacle of four thousand hits.

COUPLES
Whose wife would eat no lean?

SCIENTISTS AND INVENTORS
What invention was made possible by Thomas Edison's patent for a "means for transmitting signals electrically"?

Answers: People 63

BIBLE
His arm

TV/MOVIE STARS
Richard Chamberlain

POLITICIANS
Postmaster General

ATHLETES
St. Louis Cardinals

COUPLES
Tony and Maria

SCIENTISTS AND INVENTORS
The sewing machine

Answers: People 64

BIBLE
His head

TV/MOVIE STARS
Michael Caine

POLITICIANS
Henry Kissinger

ATHLETES
Pete Rose

COUPLES
Jack Spratt's

SCIENTISTS AND INVENTORS
Radio

People 65

BIBLE
What is the longest name in the Bible?

TV/MOVIE STARS
Born David Jones, this rock star's films include *The Man Who Fell to Earth* and *The Hunger*. What name is he known by?

POLITICIANS
What is the real middle name of Walter "Fritz" Mondale?

ATHLETES
Name the 1979 number-one draft pick of the Green Bay Packers who later sought professional help to deal with his cocaine habit.

COUPLES
Whose partner was Frank "Ponch" Poncherelli?

SCIENTISTS AND INVENTORS
True or false: Airplane co-inventor Orville Wright broke his hip and leg in a less-than-successful flight.

People 66

BIBLE
How many times does Moses hear God laugh in the Bible?

TV/MOVIE STARS
The world's most famous nanny, she went barechested in her husband's film *S.O.B.* Who is she?

POLITICIANS
Of what state was Spiro Agnew governor?

ATHLETES
Name the boxer who was known as "The Pittsburgh Kid."

COUPLES
What actor's wives have been named Sybil, Elizabeth, and Susan?

SCIENTISTS AND INVENTORS
What unit of power is named after the inventor of the steam engine?

Answers: People 65

BIBLE
Maher-shalal-hash-baz

TV/MOVIE STARS
David Bowie

POLITICIANS
Frederick

ATHLETES
Eddie Lee Ivery

COUPLES
Officer Jon Baker *(CHiPS)*

SCIENTISTS AND INVENTORS
True

Answers: People 66

BIBLE
None

TV/MOVIE STARS
Julie Andrews

POLITICIANS
Maryland

ATHLETES
Billy Conn

COUPLES
Richard Burton's

SCIENTISTS AND INVENTORS
The watt

People 67

BIBLE
Which of the following does God cause to stand still in the book of Joshua? (a) the sun (b) the moon (c) the sun and the moon

TV/MOVIE STARS
What singer-actress pioneered bell-bottomed trousers in the sixties?

POLITICIANS
Name the first lady, married in 1934, who was born Claudia Alta Taylor.

ATHLETES
Name the former Los Angeles Rams player who has made it okay for "real men" to do needlepoint.

COUPLES
To whom were Brigitte Bardot and Jane Fonda both married?

SCIENTISTS AND INVENTORS
What brought chemist Chaim Weizmann to world attention in 1948?

People 68

BIBLE
What did Aaron's serpent do to the Egyptian serpents?

TV/MOVIE STARS
True or false: Sharon Tate once made a movie entitled *The Fearless Vampire Killers or: Pardon Me, But Your Teeth are in My Neck.*

POLITICIANS
Who was Assistant to the president for National Security Affairs under Jimmy Carter?

ATHLETES
Babe Ruth hit a then-record sixty home runs in 1927. Who had held the previous record of fifty-nine home runs?

COUPLES
Of what singing duo is Daryl Dragon one half?

SCIENTISTS AND INVENTORS
What did Samuel Colt invent in 1841 by combining a mine design of Robert Fulton with research in galvanic current conducted by Robert Hare?

Answers: People 67

BIBLE
c) the sun and the moon

TV/MOVIE STARS
Cher

POLITICIANS
Lady Bird Johnson

ATHLETES
Roosevelt (Rosie) Grier

COUPLES
Roger Vadim

SCIENTISTS AND INVENTORS
He became the first president of Israel.

Answers: People 68

BIBLE
It ate them.

TV/MOVIE STARS
True

POLITICIANS
Zbigniew Brzezinksi

ATHLETES
Ruth did

COUPLES
The Captain and Tennille

SCIENTISTS AND INVENTORS
The torpedo

People 69

BIBLE
True or false: Most of the children in the Bible are named by their mothers.

TV/MOVIE STARS
What was the name of Ali McGraw's character in *Love Story*?

POLITICIANS
True or false: Adlai Stevenson fared better, vote-wise, in his second presidential race against Dwight Eisenhower than in his first.

ATHLETES
Who was the first American swimmer to win five Olympic gold medals?

COUPLES
What are the full names of the two partners on *Car 54, Where Are You*?

SCIENTISTS AND INVENTORS
Why do Silas Noble and James P. Cooley deserve the gratitude of diners the world over?

People 70

BIBLE
Through what medium is God said to have given Solomon his great wisdom?

TV/MOVIE STARS
Who did Cissy Spacek portray in *Coal Miner's Daughter*?

POLITICIANS
Name the four-term governor of New York who became an unelected vice-president.

ATHLETES
What position did the New York Yankees' Babe Ruth play?

COUPLES
What was the first name of Mrs. Slaughter on *The Mary Tyler Moore Show*?

SCIENTISTS AND INVENTORS
A Clockwork Orange made it stylish in the 1970s, but this hat had been around since James Henry Knapp invented it in 1850. Name the hat.

Answers: People 69

BIBLE
True

TV/MOVIE STARS
Jennifer (Jennie) Cavalleri

POLITICIANS
False

ATHLETES
Mark Spitz

COUPLES
Gunther Toody and Francis Muldoon

SCIENTISTS AND INVENTORS
They invented the toothpick.

Answers: People 70

BIBLE
A dream

TV/MOVIE STARS
Loretta Lynn

POLITICIANS
Nelson A. Rockefeller

ATHLETES
Right field

COUPLES
Marie

SCIENTISTS AND INVENTORS
The derby

People 71

BIBLE
What did Elisha serve at the party he threw himself when he decided to go with the prophet Elijah?

TV/MOVIE STARS
Name the onetime menace who provided the voice of Bamm Bamm Rubble in *Pebbles and Bamm Bamm*.

POLITICIANS
What title is held by the titular ruler of Tibet?

ATHLETES
In 1953, what did rookie pitcher Alvan Holloman do in his first professional game? (a) hit a home run (b) throw a no-hitter (c) give Joe DiMaggio a concussion

COUPLES
Puss Gets the Boot, in 1940, was the first cartoon to feature what legendary twosome?

SCIENTISTS AND INVENTORS
Name the French scientist who founded the modern theory of probability, and had a computer programming language named after him.

People 72

BIBLE
What was the name of Moses' wife?

TV/MOVIE STARS
Whose autobiography is *Goodness Had Nothing to Do With It*?

POLITICIANS
Name the Egyptian king forced by a military coup to abdicate in 1952.

ATHLETES
What was swimmer Cindy Nicholas the first woman to do?

COUPLES
Who is marrying Theseus in *A Midsummer Night's Dream*?

SCIENTISTS AND INVENTORS
In what field of science did Linus Pauling win his first Nobel Prize?

BIBLE
Boiled ox

TV/MOVIE STARS
Jay North

POLITICIANS
Dalai Lama

ATHLETES
b) throw a no-hitter

COUPLES
Tom and Jerry

SCIENTISTS AND INVENTORS
Blaise Pascal

BIBLE
Zipporah

TV/MOVIE STARS
Mae West

POLITICIANS
Farouk I

ATHLETES
Swim the English Channel in both directions

COUPLES
Hippolyta

SCIENTISTS AND INVENTORS
Chemistry

People 73

BIBLE
What has been fixed as Jesus' actual birthday?

TV/MOVIE STARS
The death of what actor gave Cary Grant the starring role in *Operation Petticoat*?

POLITICIANS
Name the 16th-century Englishman who conspired to blow up the Parliament.

ATHLETES
In 1963, James Warren Whittaker was the first American climber to do what?

COUPLES
By whom did Montana Wildhack have a child in *Slaughterhouse Five*?

SCIENTISTS AND INVENTORS
True or false: Laurens Hammond obtained a patent in 1932 for a bridge table that both shuffled and dealt the cards.

People 74

BIBLE
Whose sons founded the twelve Hebrew tribes?

TV/MOVIE STARS
From what did Stewart Granger change his name, since there was already a well-known actor with that moniker?

POLITICIANS
What state did Everett M. Dirksen represent in the Senate?

ATHLETES
Who was the first jockey to win $6 million in one year?

COUPLES
Who was Jacob Marley's partner?

SCIENTISTS AND INVENTORS
What did Colonel Jacob Schick patent in 1928?

BIBLE
April 3

TV/MOVIE STARS
Jeff Chandler

POLITICIANS
Guy Fawkes

ATHLETES
Scale Mount Everest

COUPLES
Billy Pilgrim

SCIENTISTS AND INVENTORS
True

Answers: People 74

BIBLE
Jacob's

TV/MOVIE STARS
James Stewart

POLITICIANS
Illinois

ATHLETES
Steve Cauthen

COUPLES
Ebeneezer Scrooge

SCIENTISTS AND INVENTORS
The electric razor

People 75

BIBLE
According to the Book of Psalms, how many chariots does God have? (a) 1 (b) 20,000 (c) "an endless number"
TV/MOVIE STARS
What actor uttered the immortal line, "I never drink—wine"?
POLITICIANS
Name the German president who appointed Hitler chancellor.
ATHLETES
Who holds the record for the most bases stolen?
COUPLES
What playwright married Charlie Chaplin's daughter, Oona?
SCIENTISTS AND INVENTORS
Name the metallic respiratory aid invented by Philip Drinker and Louis A. Shaw.

People 76

BIBLE
Samson, David, and Benaiah all performed what singular feat of strength?
TV/MOVIE STARS
Name the father and daughter who starred in *The Chalk Garden*.
POLITICIANS
Ibn Saud was the founder and first king of what nation?
ATHLETES
Who was the heaviest champion in boxing history?
COUPLES
This husband and wife team wrote *Queen Mab* and *Frankenstein*, respectively.
SCIENTISTS AND INVENTORS
Who invented the electric voting machine?

Answers: People 75

BIBLE
b) 20,000

TV/MOVIE STARS
Bela Lugosi

POLITICIANS
Paul von Hindenburg

ATHLETES
Lou Brock

COUPLES
Eugene O'Neill

SCIENTISTS AND INVENTORS
The iron lung

Answers: People 76

BIBLE
They slew a lion.

TV/MOVIE STARS
John and Haley Mills

POLITICIANS
Saudi Arabia

ATHLETES
Primo Carnera

COUPLES
Percy Bysshe Shelley and Mary Wollstonecraft Shelley

SCIENTISTS AND INVENTORS
Thomas Edison

People 77

BIBLE
To the day, how old was Noah when the rains came?

TV/MOVIE STARS
What TV newsperson wrote *The Camera Never Blinks*?

POLITICIANS
Who was Marie Antoinette's husband?

ATHLETES
Is it Jim Brown or O. J. Simpson who holds the record for the most touchdowns scored in a single season?

COUPLES
What were the first names of Beaver Clever's parents?

SCIENTISTS AND INVENTORS
What was called "Thor" because of its control of water and was invented by Alva J. Fisher in 1910?

People 78

BIBLE
True or false: John the Baptist was a teetotaler.

TV/MOVIE STARS
Name the character played by Isabel Sanford on *The Jeffersons*.

POLITICIANS
Name the Thracian gladiator who led a revolt against his Italian masters.

ATHLETES
Who had the lowest-ever score of 271 in a U.S. Masters tournament? (a) Jack Nicklaus (b) Arnold Palmer (c) Sammy Snead

COUPLES
Name the husband-wife acting team that starred in *Mission: Impossible*.

SCIENTISTS AND INVENTORS
What did a sharp young man named Joseph Glidden invent in 1873?

Answers: People 77

BIBLE
600 years, 2 months, and 17 days old

TV/MOVIE STARS
Dan Rather

POLITICIANS
Louis XVI

ATHLETES
Simpson (23)

COUPLES
June and Ward

SCIENTISTS AND INVENTORS
The washing machine

Answers: People 78

BIBLE
True

TV/MOVIE STARS
Louise Jefferson ("Weezie")

POLITICIANS
Spartacus

ATHLETES
a) Jack Nicklaus

COUPLES
Martin Landau and Barbara Bain

SCIENTISTS AND INVENTORS
Barbed wire

People 79

BIBLE
Who in Genesis was raped by his daughters?

TV/MOVIE STARS
What comedian's nickname was "Babe"?

POLITICIANS
Who was the longest reigning monarch in British history?

ATHLETES
What game, originally known as Minnonette, was invented in 1895 by William G. Morgan?

COUPLES
Who is the wife of Hiawatha?

SCIENTISTS AND INVENTORS
What item commonly used at birthdays and Christmas did Seth Wheeler patent in 1871?

People 80

BIBLE
How much did Judas receive for betraying Jesus?

TV/MOVIE STARS
What actress's best-selling autobiography was *By Myself*?

POLITICIANS
Name the Lincoln secretary of war who is thought to have had a hand in planning the assassination.

ATHLETES
Who is the only player to have put in a remarkable 26 seasons in the NFL, 1949–75?

COUPLES
Who is Tamino's lover in Mozart's *The Magic Flute*?

SCIENTISTS AND INVENTORS
What did Alexander Boardman design in 1870, erect in a New Jersey city, and name after himself?

BIBLE
Lot

TV/MOVIE STARS
Oliver Hardy

POLITICIANS
Victoria (sixty-four years)

ATHLETES
Volleyball

COUPLES
Minnehaha

SCIENTISTS AND INVENTORS
Wrapping paper

Answers: People 80

BIBLE
Thirty sheckels

TV/MOVIE STARS
Lauren Bacall

POLITICIANS
Edwin M. Stanton

ATHLETES
George Blanda

COUPLES
Pamina

SCIENTISTS AND INVENTORS
The boardwalk

People 81

BIBLE
On what part of the body were slaves of Hebrew masters marked? (a) the sole (b) the ear (c) the palm

TV/MOVIE STARS
True or false: Burt Lancaster was a mine worker before becoming an actor.

POLITICIANS
Was Genghis Khan the grandson or grandfather of Kublai Khan?

ATHLETES
"Duffy's Cliff," named after the player who worked there, refers to the outfield of what stadium?

COUPLES
In the videogame, who is the inamorata of Donkey Kong's Mario?

SCIENTISTS AND INVENTORS
How many elements were discovered by cave dwellers?

People 82

BIBLE
With what did King Saul try to kill David?

TV/MOVIE STARS
Who played Olive Oyl in the 1980 film *Popeye*?

POLITICIANS
Name the women's rights activist who teamed with Elizabeth Cady Stanton to found the newspaper *The Revolution*.

ATHLETES
What was the better-known name of heavyweight champion Arnold Raymond Cream?

COUPLES
Who was the mistress of Dr. Zhivago?

SCIENTISTS AND INVENTORS
Stafford, Slayton, and Brand were the crew of the last Apollo flight. What was its distinction?

Answers: People 81

BIBLE
b) the ear

TV/MOVIE STARS
False. He was a circus acrobat.

POLITICIANS
Grandfather

ATHLETES
Fenway Park

COUPLES
Pauline

SCIENTISTS AND INVENTORS
Ten (gold, iron, mercury, carbon, copper, lead, silver, sulfur, tin, and zinc)

Answers: People 82

BIBLE
A spear

TV/MOVIE STARS
Shelley Duvall

POLITICIANS
Susan B. Anthony

ATHLETES
Jersey Joe Walcott

COUPLES
Lara

SCIENTISTS AND INVENTORS
It docked in space with a Russian ship.

People 83

BIBLE
Judith's grandfather had the same name as what animal?

TV/MOVIE STARS
Who played James Bond between Sean Connery and Roger Moore?

POLITICIANS
Who was the dictator of Spain from 1937–75?

ATHLETES
Who took the silver in Women's Figure Skating in the 1980 Olympics?

COUPLES
Who is Larry Hagman's famous mother?

SCIENTISTS AND INVENTORS
True or false: G. H. Darwin, scientist-son of Charles, followed in his father's footsteps and became a naturalist.

People 84

BIBLE
Which one of these was not punishable by death?   (a) working on the Sabbath   (b) lying about being a virgin   (c) bringing an animal into a temple

TV/MOVIE STARS
What is the name of Robert Redford's resort in the Utah mountains?

POLITICIANS
What does the *M* stand for in Alexander M. Haig?

ATHLETES
True or false: Babe Ruth was a coach with the Brooklyn Dodgers after he retired from active playing.

COUPLES
Name the stars who met on the set of *Clash of the Titans* in 1981, and had a child together.

SCIENTISTS AND INVENTORS
True or false: The Leonid meteor shower is so named in honor of the Russian scientist who discovered it.

Answers: People 83

BIBLE
Ox

TV/MOVIE STARS
George Lazenby

POLITICIANS
Francisco Franco

ATHLETES
Linda Fratianne

COUPLES
Mary Martin

SCIENTISTS AND INVENTORS
False. He became an astronomer.

Answers: People 84

BIBLE
c) bringing an animal into a temple

TV/MOVIE STARS
Sundance

POLITICIANS
Meigs

ATHLETES
True

COUPLES
Harry Hamlin and Ursula Andress

SCIENTISTS AND INVENTORS
False. The shower is so-named because it radiates from the constellation Leo.

People 85

BIBLE
True or false: Sheba was beheaded.

TV/MOVIE STARS
Whose remarks about "Zionist hoodlums" during the 1977 Oscars saw her all but pelted with vegetables by the outraged audience?

POLITICIANS
Hammurabi, author of the great and ancient codes, was king of what empire?

ATHLETES
Harry Greb handed what boxer his only professional defeat?

COUPLES
Name the Englishman whose execution was prevented by the Indian maiden Pocahontas.

SCIENTISTS AND INVENTORS
Who invented the bifocal lens?

People 86

BIBLE
What additional torment was suffered by the thieves who were crucified with Jesus?

TV/MOVIE STARS
What film did Richard Dreyfuss quit in a snit, leaving the part and subsequent Oscar nomination to Roy Scheider?

POLITICIANS
What New York mayor was known as "The Little Flower"?

ATHLETES
From what team did the New York Yankees obtain Roger Maris?

COUPLES
Who teamed with James Garner in a series of popular Polaroid TV commercials?

SCIENTISTS AND INVENTORS
It took some time, but what did Christiaan Huygens finally invent in 1656?

Answers: People 85

BIBLE
True

TV/MOVIE STARS
Vanessa Redgrave's

POLITICIANS
The Babylonian Empire

ATHLETES
Gene Tunney

COUPLES
Captain John Smith

SCIENTISTS AND INVENTORS
Benjamin Franklin

Answers: People 86

BIBLE
Their legs were broken.

TV/MOVIE STARS
All That Jazz

POLITICIANS
Fiorello LaGuardia

ATHLETES
The Kansas City A's

COUPLES
Mariette Hartley

SCIENTISTS AND INVENTORS
A clock

People 87

BIBLE
How long did Delilah weep to persuade Samson to give her the answer to a riddle?   (a) an hour   (b) a day   (c) a week

TV/MOVIE STARS
Name the two science-fiction heroes played by Buster Crabbe.

POLITICIANS
Name the Democratic senator who sought his party's nomination for president based almost entirely on his opposition to the Vietnam War.

ATHLETES
Name the restaurant Pete Rozelle forced Joe Namath to sell in 1969.

COUPLES
They were born Leonard Slye and Frances Octavia Smith. What are the better-known names of this husband-wife acting team?

SCIENTISTS AND INVENTORS
Who came up with vulcanized rubber in 1839?

People 88

BIBLE
To whom did David speak his last words?

TV/MOVIE STARS
Who was the first member of the original *Saturday Night Live* troupe to leave the show?

POLITICIANS
Activist Malcolm Little was better known by what name?

ATHLETES
In 1970, Diane Crump was the first woman to participate in what sporting event?

COUPLES
Petruchio and Katharina are the hot-tempered lovers of what play?

SCIENTISTS AND INVENTORS
Who invented the telegraph?

Answers: People 87

BIBLE
c) a week

TV/MOVIE STARS
Flash Gordon and Buck Rogers

POLITICIANS
Eugene McCarthy

ATHLETES
Bachelors III

COUPLES
Roy Rogers and Dale Evans

SCIENTISTS AND INVENTORS
Charles Goodyear

Answers: People 88

BIBLE
Solomon

TV/MOVIE STARS
Chevy Chase

POLITICIANS
Malcolm X

ATHLETES
The Kentucky Derby

COUPLES
The Taming of the Shrew

SCIENTISTS AND INVENTORS
Samuel F. B. Morse

People 89

BIBLE
What does John say were the last words of Jesus?

TV/MOVIE STARS
What best-selling novelist played Walt Disney's TV hero Texas John Slaughter?

POLITICIANS
Name the Aztec emperor who was slain for opposing Cortes.

ATHLETES
Who quarterbacked the Baltimore Colts when Johnny Unitas was injured in 1968?

COUPLES
Who does Lucie end up with in *A Tale of Two Cities*: Sydney Carton or Charles Darnay?

SCIENTISTS AND INVENTORS
Who invented the forerunner of the hand grenade and gave his name to its issue?

People 90

BIBLE
True or false: Jesus used spit to cure a blind man.

TV/MOVIE STARS
Who played Lando Calrissian in *The Empire Strikes Back* and *Return of the Jedi*?

POLITICIANS
Who was nicknamed "Il Duce"?

ATHLETES
Name the athlete who took the gold in the 1976 Olympics for Women's Figure Skating.

COUPLES
Name the pope who was Michelangelo's long-suffering patron.

SCIENTISTS AND INVENTORS
Whose prize invention was dynamite?

BIBLE
"It is finished."

TV/MOVIE STARS
Tom Tryon

POLITICIANS
Montezuma

ATHLETES
Earl Morrall

COUPLES
Charles Darnay

SCIENTISTS AND INVENTORS
Henry Shrapnel

Answers: People 90

BIBLE
True

TV/MOVIE STARS
Billy Dee Williams

POLITICIANS
Benito Mussolini

ATHLETES
Dorothy Hamill

COUPLES
Pope Julius II

SCIENTISTS AND INVENTORS
Alfred B. Nobel

People 91

BIBLE
What bore Elijah to heaven?

TV/MOVIE STARS
How many times did Barbra Streisand play Fanny Brice in the movies?

POLITICIANS
Simon Bolivar cut a swath across much of South America in opposition to what nation's rule?

ATHLETES
After breaking the "color barrier," what did Jackie Robinson do his first time at bat?   (a) hit a home run   (b) strike out   (c) walk

COUPLES
To whom was James Bond briefly married?

SCIENTISTS AND INVENTORS
The company that bears his name makes office machines, but in 1885 he had only invented the adding machine. Who was he?

People 92

BIBLE
Who was Moses' father-in-law?

TV/MOVIE STARS
True or false: Years before he became *Star Trek*'s Mr. Spock, Leonard Nimoy played an extraterrestrial in *Zombies of the Stratosphere*.

POLITICIANS
True or false: Spiro Agnew was the first vice-president to resign.

ATHLETES
John W. Heisman, for whom the Heisman trophy is named, spent thirty-six years serving football in what capacity?

COUPLES
According to Greek mythology, where did Orpheus travel in the futile attempt to recover his beloved wife Eurydice?

SCIENTISTS AND INVENTORS
What invention was the work of Elisha G. Otis?

Answers: People 91

BIBLE
A whirlwind

TV/MOVIE STARS
Twice. In *Funny Girl* and *Funny Lady*.

POLITICIANS
Spain's

ATHLETES
b) strike out

COUPLES
Tracy

SCIENTISTS AND INVENTORS
William Burroughs

Answers: People 92

BIBLE
Jethro

TV/MOVIE STARS
True

POLITICIANS
False. John C. Calhoun left the office to become a senator in 1832.

ATHLETES
As a college coach

COUPLES
The underworld (Hades)

SCIENTISTS AND INVENTORS
The elevator

People 93

BIBLE
Exhibiting the guts of a one-man army, what did lone Razis toss at the five hundred enemy soldiers sent to kill him?

TV/MOVIE STARS
Name the character Lloyd Bridges played in *Sea Hunt*.

POLITICIANS
Walter Mondale was a devoted protegé of what Minnesota senator?

ATHLETES
True or false: No player has ever died as a result of injuries suffered in a National Hockey League game.

COUPLES
From what actor did *Laverne & Shirley*'s Penny Marshall separate in 1979?

SCIENTISTS AND INVENTORS
Although Leonardo da Vinci designed a working model of this vehicle, it remained for Paul Cornu to figure out, in 1907, how to make one work with a passenger inside. What's the invention?

People 94

BIBLE
Of what group was God speaking when he said, "I will give them an everlasting name, that shall not be cut off"?

TV/MOVIE STARS
Who played Nellie Forbush in the film version of *South Pacific*?

POLITICIANS
Who is frequently referred to as "the first Lady President"?

ATHLETES
Who was the first professional golfer to earn more than $100,000 in a season?

COUPLES
True or false: Husband and wife Paula Prentiss and Dick Benjamin once played husband and wife in a TV sitcom.

SCIENTISTS AND INVENTORS
Edison invented one that was cylindrical, but it is Peter Goldmark's flat version we use today. What plastic article is being discussed?

Answers: People 93

BIBLE
His own intestines

TV/MOVIE STARS
Mike Nelson

POLITICIANS
Hubert Humphrey

ATHLETES
False. Minnesota North Stars player Bill Masterton died of head injuries in 1968.

COUPLES
Rob Reiner (*All in the Family*)

SCIENTISTS AND INVENTORS
The helicopter

Answers: People 94

BIBLE
Eunuchs

TV/MOVIE STARS
Mitzi Gaynor

POLITICIANS
Mrs. Edith Wilson, who stood in for Woodrow after his stroke.

ATHLETES
Arnold Palmer

COUPLES
True. The show was *He & She*.

SCIENTISTS AND INVENTORS
The phonograph record

People 95

BIBLE
How many times does Matthew call the Magi "kings"?

TV/MOVIE STARS
True or false: Noel Neill, who played Lois Lane on the *Superman* TV show, is seen briefly as Lois Lane's mother in the 1978 motion picture *Superman*.

POLITICIANS
Who was president before Abraham Lincoln?

ATHLETES
In 1877, Spencer Gore was the first player to win what tournament?

COUPLES
Name the son and daughter of two *Wizard of Oz* stars who were married from 1974–78.

SCIENTISTS AND INVENTORS
Who invented polarizing glass, i.e., Polaroid?

People 96

BIBLE
What was Amos the only prophet ever to report seeing in God's hands?

TV/MOVIE STARS
Who played Lon Chaney, Sr., in the biographical film *Man of a Thousand Faces*?

POLITICIANS
For the welfare of what group did activist Dorothea Dix campaign vigorously?

ATHLETES
What water sport was invented, though never tried, by Benjamin Franklin?

COUPLES
Who was Ronald Reagan's first wife?

SCIENTISTS AND INVENTORS
Did Edwin Armstrong invent AM or FM broadcasting?

BIBLE
None. He refers to them only as "wise men."

TV/MOVIE STARS
True

POLITICIANS
James Buchanan

ATHLETES
Wimbledon

COUPLES
Liza Minnelli and Jack Haley, Jr.

SCIENTISTS AND INVENTORS
Edwin H. Land

Answers: People 96

BIBLE
A plumbline

TV/MOVIE STARS
James Cagney

POLITICIANS
The mentally ill

ATHLETES
Waterskiing

COUPLES
Jane Wyman

SCIENTISTS AND INVENTORS
FM broadcasting

People 97

BIBLE
What was the name of the angel who told Mary that she was to carry God's son?

TV/MOVIE STARS
In what film did Katharine Ross get to play a woman and her robot duplicate?

POLITICIANS
What was the more familiar name of corrupt New York political leader William M. Tweed?

ATHLETES
Who won the first welterweight championship bout between Roberto Duran and Sugar Ray Leonard?

COUPLES
In whose arms did actress Diana Hyland finally succumb to cancer?

SCIENTISTS AND INVENTORS
Who was the last astronaut to fly in the *Mercury* program?

People 98

BIBLE
What did Jonah wear on his head while he was in the belly of the whale?

TV/MOVIE STARS
Who was typecast as a film director in *Sunset Boulevard*?

POLITICIANS
Of what nation was Ian Smith prime minister?

ATHLETES
What baseball player was known as "The Bird"?

COUPLES
Hollywood boycotted Ingrid Bergman when she left her husband and daughter to live with what film director?

SCIENTISTS AND INVENTORS
What nationality was the first astronaut who was not Russian or American?

BIBLE
Gabriel

TV/MOVIE STARS
The Stepford Wives

POLITICIANS
Boss Tweed

ATHLETES
Duran

COUPLES
John Travolta's

SCIENTISTS AND INVENTORS
L. Gordon Cooper

Answers: People 98

BIBLE
Weeds

TV/MOVIE STARS
Cecil B. DeMille

POLITICIANS
Rhodesia

ATHLETES
Mark Fidrych

COUPLES
Roberto Rossellini

SCIENTISTS AND INVENTORS
Czechoslovakian. He flew on board Russia's *Soyuz XXVIII*.

People 99

BIBLE
How was Lot related to Abraham?

TV/MOVIE STARS
True or false: Steve McQueen was the star of *The Blob*.

POLITICIANS
What was the Mexican revolutionary and bandit Doroteo Arango better known as?

ATHLETES
Who did Floyd Patterson beat to win his first heavyweight boxing title?

COUPLES
Who shares a comic strip with "Hi"?

SCIENTISTS AND INVENTORS
What controversial procedure did Dr. John Dalton begin practicing on animals in 1855 to show "the living process of life"?

People 100

BIBLE
With what slippery substance did Job wash his steps?

TV/MOVIE STARS
What president did Jason Robards play in *The Legend of the Lone Ranger*?

POLITICIANS
True or false: The "Taft" of the Taft-Hartley Labor Act is President William Howard Taft.

ATHLETES
What was the first tournament won by Jack Nicklaus?

COUPLES
What brother and sister pair have helped teach generations of children to read?

SCIENTISTS AND INVENTORS
In 1889, Amos Alonzo Stagg took a gym mat and improvised what now-common piece of football paraphernalia?

Answers: People 99

BIBLE
Lot was Abraham's nephew.

TV/MOVIE STARS
True

POLITICIANS
Pancho Villa

ATHLETES
Archie Moore

COUPLES
Lois

SCIENTISTS AND INVENTORS
Vivisection

Answers: People 100

BIBLE
Butter

TV/MOVIE STARS
Ulysses S. Grant

POLITICIANS
False. Senator Robert A. Taft

ATHLETES
The U.S. Open (1962)

COUPLES
Dick and Jane

SCIENTISTS AND INVENTORS
The football dummy

PART FOUR

LEISURE ACTIVITIES

Leisure Activities 1

ENTERTAINMENT
How many members of the Three Stooges have there been?
SPORTS
Where will the 1988 Summer Olympics be held?
GAMES
How many different color wedges are there in *Trivial Pursuit*?
FOOD AND DRINK
What was Ephraim Wales Bull's contribution to wine?
HEALTH AND FITNESS
Name the national medical plan introduced in 1966
TRAVEL
Where would you be if you saw a green flag with a red circle in the center?

Leisure Activities 2

ENTERTAINMENT
What is the name of the musical in Mel Brooks's *The Producers*?
SPORTS
In what city did Harold Abrahams and Eric Liddell, the *Chariots of Fire* runners, race in the 1924 Olympics?
GAMES
What are the names of the three light blue deeds in *Monopoly*?
FOOD AND DRINK
What is Austria's Kaisersemmeln?
HEALTH AND FITNESS
What is an enlargement of the thyroid gland called?
TRAVEL
What American state is surrounded on three sides by another country?

Answers: Leisure Activities 1

ENTERTAINMENT
Six. Moe, Curly, Shemp, Larry and two Joes.

SPORTS
Seoul, South Korea

GAMES
Six

FOOD AND DRINK
He developed the concord grape.

HEALTH AND FITNESS
Medicare

TRAVEL
Bangladesh

Answers: Leisure Activities 2

ENTERTAINMENT
Springtime for Hitler

SPORTS
Paris

GAMES
Connecticut, Vermont, and Oriental Avenues

FOOD AND DRINK
A roll

HEALTH AND FITNESS
A goiter

TRAVEL
Maine

Leisure Activities 3

ENTERTAINMENT
What 1960's TV character worked for Spacely Space Sprockets, Inc.?

SPORTS
Who was the only player to hit All Star Game home runs in three consecutive years?

GAMES
Name the Parker Brothers game in which players seek units in money, fame, and happiness.

FOOD AND DRINK
What was Julia Child's first cookbook?

HEALTH AND FITNESS
What vitamin do we get from liver, wheat, yeast, and meat?

TRAVEL
When it's eight P.M. in Moscow, what time is it in New York?

Leisure Activities 4

ENTERTAINMENT
Name the Bulwer-Litton novel that was a 1984 miniseries.

SPORTS
What renowned race, when first held in 1897, was won by John J. McDermott?

GAMES
What do players conquer in *Risk*?   (a) the world   (b) a castle   (c) The Milky Way

FOOD AND DRINK
What is the scientific name for NutraSweet?

HEALTH AND FITNESS
What part of the body is affected by Bell's Palsy?

TRAVEL
Moving due south from the bottom-most point of Greenland, what is the first country a traveler will reach?

Answers: Leisure Activities 3

ENTERTAINMENT
George Jetson

SPORTS
Al Kaline

GAMES
Careers

FOOD AND DRINK
Mastering the Art of French Cooking

HEALTH AND FITNESS
Niacin (Nicotinic acid)

TRAVEL
Twelve noon

Answers: Leisure Activities 4

ENTERTAINMENT
The Last Days of Pompeii

SPORTS
The Boston Marathon

GAMES
a) the world

FOOD AND DRINK
Aspartame

HEALTH AND FITNESS
The face

TRAVEL
Brazil

Leisure Activities 5

ENTERTAINMENT
True or false: *The Black Cauldron* will be Walt Disney's twenty-fifth animated feature.

SPORTS
Gold medalist Richard Fosbury introduced what unique high-jump style in the 1968 Olympics?

GAMES
How many suspects are in a game of *Clue*?

FOOD AND DRINK
In what is Chinese cuisine braised?

HEALTH AND FITNESS
What vitamin is essential for the normal clotting of blood?

TRAVEL
Passing west over the International Date Line, does a traveler gain or lose a day?

Leisure Activities 6

ENTERTAINMENT
Who made the Robinson Family's spaceship fly off course in the 1960s TV series *Lost in Space*?

SPORTS
True or false: One form of martial arts trains its adherents to dodge bullets.

GAMES
What is the mustachioed *Monopoly* mascot holding on the Community Chest "Get Out of Jail, Free" card?

FOOD AND DRINK
What is the native name for Mexican tripe soup?

HEALTH AND FITNESS
Which blood pressure would be of more concern to your doctor: 160/85 or 145/95?

TRAVEL
How many states are touched by California?

Answers: Leisure Activities 5

ENTERTAINMENT
True

SPORTS
The Fosbury Flop

GAMES
Six

FOOD AND DRINK
Soy sauce

HEALTH AND FITNESS
Vitamin K

TRAVEL
Gain

Answers: Leisure Activities 6

ENTERTAINMENT
Dr. Zachary Smith

SPORTS
False

GAMES
A cane

FOOD AND DRINK
Menudo

HEALTH AND FITNESS
145/95. Elevation of the diastolic pressure is a more ominous sign.

TRAVEL
Three: Oregon, Nevada, and Arizona.

Leisure Activities 7

ENTERTAINMENT
The death of what actress on July 8, 1967, was marked in London with the dousing of all outside lights at West End theaters?

SPORTS
What is the name of the throwing equipment that has a metal head, a wire handle, and a grip?

GAMES
For what does the abbreviation "D & D" stand?

FOOD AND DRINK
True or false: Metal pots or pans cannot be used in a microwave oven.

HEALTH AND FITNESS
Where in the body is insulin manufactured?

TRAVEL
Which state has the most miles of hiking trails?

Leisure Activities 8

ENTERTAINMENT
Who played TV's Tarzan?

SPORTS
What is a "rhubarb" in baseball?

GAMES
With one house how much is the rental on *Monopoly*'s Boardwalk?

FOOD AND DRINK
Which contains more calories, an average-sized banana or apple?

HEALTH AND FITNESS
Eating too much salt increases one's risk of developing what ailment?

TRAVEL
Where is Kai Tak airport?

Answers: Leisure Activities 7

ENTERTAINMENT
Vivien Leigh

SPORTS
The hammer

GAMES
Dungeons & Dragons

FOOD AND DRINK
True

HEALTH AND FITNESS
The pancreas

TRAVEL
California

Answers: Leisure Activities 8

ENTERTAINMENT
Ron Ely

SPORTS
An argument, usually heated

GAMES
$200

FOOD AND DRINK
Banana

HEALTH AND FITNESS
High blood pressure

TRAVEL
In Hong Kong

Leisure Activities 9

ENTERTAINMENT
Who was the first conductor of radio's NBC symphony?
SPORTS
What city hosted the 1936 Summer Olympics?
GAMES
How many red-letter cubes are in *Perquackey*?
FOOD AND DRINK
What famous Chinese dish is known as Tsa Siu in Mandarin?
HEALTH AND FITNESS
What is the name for the upper portion of the brain?
TRAVEL
Which two states does Memphis, Tennessee, adjoin?

Leisure Activities 10

ENTERTAINMENT
What Off-Broadway smash was based on a 1960 Roger Corman horror film?
SPORTS
What team won the World Series on October 16, 1969?
GAMES
How many letters are drawn to begin play in *Scrabble*?
FOOD AND DRINK
Is loquat a fruit, a vegetable, or candy?
HEALTH AND FITNESS
What two organs are most affected by alcohol?
TRAVEL
What two American states are surrounded on three sides by water?

Answers: Leisure Activities 9

ENTERTAINMENT
Arturo Toscanini

SPORTS
Berlin

GAMES
Three

FOOD AND DRINK
Chop suey

HEALTH AND FITNESS
The cerebrum

TRAVEL
Arkansas and Mississippi

Answers: Leisure Activities 10

ENTERTAINMENT
Little Shop of Horrors

SPORTS
The New York Mets

GAMES
Seven

FOOD AND DRINK
A fruit

HEALTH AND FITNESS
The brain and liver

TRAVEL
Florida and Alaska

Leisure Activities 11

ENTERTAINMENT
What famous jungle character did Johnny Weismueller play after hanging up his Tarzan loincloth?

SPORTS
In what country will the 1988 Winter Olympics be held?

GAMES
What board game features "Shlemazel" cards?

FOOD AND DRINK
What is the more familiar name of Enchiladas de Queso?

HEALTH AND FITNESS
What does a pogonophobic fear?

TRAVEL
South Korea is sided by what three bodies of water?

Leisure Activities 12

ENTERTAINMENT
What does the MGM motto "Ars Gratia Artis" mean?

SPORTS
What is a "kiai" in martial arts?

GAMES
What game was the first to be packaged with the ColecoVision master component?

FOOD AND DRINK
The Turkish dish chicken borek is a chicken-filled what?

HEALTH AND FITNESS
What is the normal body temperature—in Centigrade?

TRAVEL
What is the main airport in Sydney, Australia?

Answers: Leisure Activities 11

ENTERTAINMENT
Jungle Jim

SPORTS
Canada

GAMES
Chutzpah

FOOD AND DRINK
Cheese enchiladas

HEALTH AND FITNESS
Beards

TRAVEL
Yellow Sea, Sea of Japan, and East China Sea

Answers: Leisure Activities 12

ENTERTAINMENT
"Art for Art's Sake"

SPORTS
A shout of self-assertion

GAMES
Donkey Kong

FOOD AND DRINK
Bun

HEALTH AND FITNESS
37 degrees

TRAVEL
Sydney International Airport

Leisure Activities 13

ENTERTAINMENT
Who wrote the classic play *The Trojan Women*?

SPORTS
In the 1932 World Series, which batter pointed deep into center field, then sent the ball soaring over the fence at that exact spot?

GAMES
What was the name of the 1982 Odyssey series in which games were played on a traditional board while battles were fought using video games?

FOOD AND DRINK
What is the name for a Mexican dish made with minced, seasoned meat packed in cornmeal dough, wrapped in corn husks, and steamed?

HEALTH AND FITNESS
Which, hour for hour, consumes the most calories? (a) rowing (b) snooker (c) tennis

TRAVEL
True or false: The prime meridian passes through Africa.

Leisure Activities 14

ENTERTAINMENT
True or false: Black Beauty was an all-black horse.

SPORTS
Before he changed his name, Muhammad Ali was Cassius Clay. What was Clay's middle name?

GAMES
Name the game that originated in India and features a board with "Home" in the center and a "Start" in each corner?

FOOD AND DRINK
Which is the "red" clam chowder, Manhattan or New England?

HEALTH AND FITNESS
True or false: A child's normal body temperature is slightly lower than an adult's.

TRAVEL
What was John F. Kennedy International Airport called before its name was changed?

Answers: Leisure Activities 13

ENTERTAINMENT
Euripides

SPORTS
Babe Ruth

GAMES
Master Strategy series

FOOD AND DRINK
Tamale

HEALTH AND FITNESS
a) rowing

TRAVEL
True

Answers: Leisure Activities 14

ENTERTAINMENT
False. Black Beauty had a white star on his forehead.

SPORTS
Marcellus

GAMES
Parcheesi

FOOD AND DRINK
Manhattan

HEALTH AND FITNESS
False. It's slightly higher.

TRAVEL
Idlewild

Leisure Activities 15

ENTERTAINMENT
Name the bellhop played by Bill Dana on his 1963–65 NBC sitcom.

SPORTS
What is football commissioner Pete Rozelle's first name?

GAMES
In what classic Milton Bradley game do players get married, raise children, buy homes and autos, take out life insurance and, if they wish, play the stock market?

FOOD AND DRINK
What kind of wine is Edelzwicker?

HEALTH AND FITNESS
Are deciduous teeth the "baby" or "adult" set?

TRAVEL
Does the hammer face left or right on the Soviet flag?

Leisure Activities 16

ENTERTAINMENT
Name the popular Italian singer who dyed her hair purple before touring the U.S.—in 1859!

SPORTS
Early in his career, what golfer was nicknamed the "Golden Bear"?

GAMES
Name the game played by Death and the Knight in the film *The Seventh Seal*.

FOOD AND DRINK
Which one of these is *not* a means of heating Chinese chafing dishes? (a) charcoal (b) water (c) alcohol

HEALTH AND FITNESS
In general, do men or women have a more rapid pulse rate?

TRAVEL
What is the currency of Guatemala?

Answers: Leisure Activities 15

ENTERTAINMENT
Jose Jimenez

SPORTS
Alvin

GAMES
The Game of Life

FOOD AND DRINK
A white wine blended from two different kinds of grapes

HEALTH AND FITNESS
Baby

TRAVEL
Left

Answers: Leisure Activities 16

ENTERTAINMENT
Adelina Patti

SPORTS
Jack Nicklaus

GAMES
Chess

FOOD AND DRINK
b) water

HEALTH AND FITNESS
Women

TRAVEL
The quetzal

Leisure Activities 17

ENTERTAINMENT
Phileas Fogg was the hero of what novel?

SPORTS
What is the length of each period in hockey?

GAMES
True or false: When flipping baseball cards, if a "leaner" is knocked down, the card is disqualified.

FOOD AND DRINK
The eggs of what sturgeon are the preferred form of caviar?

HEALTH AND FITNESS
True or false: The incubation period for leprosy can span several years.

TRAVEL
How many time zones are there in South America?

Leisure Activities 18

ENTERTAINMENT
Adrienne Barbeau and Barry Bostwick, then unknowns, were the stars of what long-running Broadway musical when it opened in February, 1972?

SPORTS
True or false: Badminton got its name from the hall in which it was developed.

GAMES
What are the six categories of the Genus edition of *Trivial Pursuit*™?

FOOD AND DRINK
What is called "The Breakfast of Champions"?

HEALTH AND FITNESS
What part of the eye is stored in eye banks?

TRAVEL
Where is Haneda International Airport?

Answers: Leisure Activities 17

ENTERTAINMENT
Around the World in Eighty Days

SPORTS
Twenty minutes

GAMES
False. It is counted in its new position.

FOOD AND DRINK
The beluga (white sturgeon)

HEALTH AND FITNESS
True

TRAVEL
Three

Answers: Leisure Activities 18

ENTERTAINMENT
Grease

SPORTS
True

GAMES
Geography, Entertainment, History, Art and Literature, Science and Nature, and Sports and Leisure.

FOOD AND DRINK
Wheaties

HEALTH AND FITNESS
The cornea

TRAVEL
Tokyo

Leisure Activities 19

ENTERTAINMENT
What is the name of Brody's wife in *Jaws*?

SPORTS
From what kind of wood are bowling pins made?

GAMES
The "running game" and the "back game" are basic strategies in what popular game?

FOOD AND DRINK
Which company's cookies are "made by elves"?

HEALTH AND FITNESS
What is measured in terms of systolic and diastolic?

TRAVEL
True or false: The equator slices Japan in two.

Leisure Activities 20

ENTERTAINMENT
In the title of the Pulitzer Prize-winning play, to what were Man-in-the-Moon Marigolds exposed?

SPORTS
How high from the court is a basketball hoop?

GAMES
What 1960s Transogram game came with a plastic "answer phone"?

FOOD AND DRINK
Which contains more calories, a Saltine or a slice of Melba toast?

HEALTH AND FITNESS
If you suffer from linonophobia, what do you fear?

TRAVEL
True or false: London and Paris are in different time zones.

Answers: Leisure Activities 19

ENTERTAINMENT
Ellen

SPORTS
Maple

GAMES
Backgammon

FOOD AND DRINK
Keebler's

HEALTH AND FITNESS
Blood pressure

TRAVEL
False

Answers: Leisure Activities 20

ENTERTAINMENT
Gamma rays

SPORTS
Ten feet

GAMES
Miss Popularity Game

FOOD AND DRINK
Melba toast

HEALTH AND FITNESS
String

TRAVEL
True

Leisure Activities 21

ENTERTAINMENT
In what 1981 Pulitzer Prize winning play does a character claim to have offered her husband lemonade after shooting him?

SPORTS
What's another name for a "screen" in basketball?

GAMES
In board-gaming, what is an "orthogonal" move?

FOOD AND DRINK
Gulyas soup is a delicacy of what country?

HEALTH AND FITNESS
"Chemother." is the abbreviation for what medical procedure?

TRAVEL
Is Havana on the east or west side of Cuba?

Leisure Activities 22

ENTERTAINMENT
The full title of the musical is?   (a) *Hello, Dolly!*   (b) *Hello Dolly!*   (c) *Hello Dolly*

SPORTS
How many balls are used in billiards?

GAMES
What tile grouping in *Ma-Jong* contains the Red, White, and Green Dragons?

FOOD AND DRINK
For what additive does the abbreviation MSG stand?

HEALTH AND FITNESS
Gamophobia is a fear of what?

TRAVEL
What is the only nation with a one-color flag?

ENTERTAINMENT
Crimes of the Heart

SPORTS
A pick

GAMES
A move along a rank or file

FOOD AND DRINK
Hungary

HEALTH AND FITNESS
Chemotherapy

TRAVEL
West

ENTERTAINMENT
a) *Hello, Dolly!*

SPORTS
Sixteen. Fifteen numbered, plus the cue ball.

GAMES
Cardinal tiles

FOOD AND DRINK
Monosodium Glutamate

HEALTH AND FITNESS
Marriage

TRAVEL
Libya (green)

Leisure Activities 23

ENTERTAINMENT
What is the most expensive music video ever made?

SPORTS
What, in bowling, are "bedposts"?

GAMES
What is the shape of the board in Byzantine chess?   (a) square   (b) circular   (c) triangular

FOOD AND DRINK
Whey is the water part of what?

HEALTH AND FITNESS
What is a comminuted fracture?

TRAVEL
Which city is further south, London or Moscow?

Leisure Activities 24

ENTERTAINMENT
What's the name of both the play that starred Julie Andrews and the movie that starred Audrey Hepburn?

SPORTS
Where do boxers strike when using the illegal "rabbit punch"?

GAMES
Draughts is the English name for what game?

FOOD AND DRINK
In Jewish cuisine, what are latkes?

HEALTH AND FITNESS
True or false: Cataracts are a normal consequence of aging.

TRAVEL
What country lies both north and west of the Falkland Islands?

Answers: Leisure Activities 23

ENTERTAINMENT
Michael Jackson's *Thriller*

SPORTS
7-10 splits

GAMES
b) circular

FOOD AND DRINK
Milk

HEALTH AND FITNESS
One in which the bone is broken in several places

TRAVEL
London

Answers: Leisure Activities 24

ENTERTAINMENT
My Fair Lady

SPORTS
The back of the neck

GAMES
Checkers

FOOD AND DRINK
Pancakes

HEALTH AND FITNESS
False. They're a common problem but not considered normal.

TRAVEL
Argentina

Leisure Activities 25

ENTERTAINMENT
Who is the lead singer of Jefferson Starship?
SPORTS
In a football blitz, who joins the linemen in rushing the passer?
GAMES
How many numbered squares are there on a Bingo card?
FOOD AND DRINK
Carob is a nutritious, increasingly popular substitute for what food?
HEALTH AND FITNESS
What kind of bone is the Atlas?
TRAVEL
What is the more familiar name of Tutuila Island?

Leisure Activities 26

ENTERTAINMENT
What literary and cinematic figure is adored by Miss Moneypenny?
SPORTS
Which of these golf terms signifies one stroke over par?   (a) bogey   (b) birdie   (c) dub
GAMES
What is "the game that ties you up in knots"?
FOOD AND DRINK
Which oil has the mildest flavor of the unrefined oils?
HEALTH AND FITNESS
Which is higher in iron, peas or tomatoes?
TRAVEL
Is the island of Tasmania north or south of Australia?

Answers: Leisure Activities 25

ENTERTAINMENT
Grace Slick

SPORTS
One or more defensive backs

GAMES
Twenty-four (the one in the center is Free)

FOOD AND DRINK
Chocolate

HEALTH AND FITNESS
A vertebra (the first just below the skull)

TRAVEL
American Samoa

Answers: Leisure Activities 26

ENTERTAINMENT
James Bond

SPORTS
a) bogey

GAMES
Twister

FOOD AND DRINK
Safflower oil

HEALTH AND FITNESS
Peas, by a factor of four-to-one.

TRAVEL
South

Leisure Activities 27

ENTERTAINMENT
Name the family of writers responsible for *The Book of Lists* and its sequels.

SPORTS
In hockey, what parts of the body are used for body checking?

GAMES
Apart from a board and pegs, what is needed to play cribbage?

FOOD AND DRINK
What beverage did Galileo describe as "light held together by water"?

HEALTH AND FITNESS
What are the brachialis and brachioradialis?

TRAVEL
True or false: The New Taiwan Dollar is equal to the U.S. dollar.

Leisure Activities 28

ENTERTAINMENT
Who played Tonto on *The Lone Ranger* TV series?

SPORTS
What is a racehorse if it's the "chalk horse"?

GAMES
What kind of game is *Balls!*?

FOOD AND DRINK
From what is the applesauce dye carmine derived?

HEALTH AND FITNESS
True or false: Saigon Cinnamon is used to combat intestinal gas.

TRAVEL
What time is it in London when it is seven P.M. in Peking?

Answers: Leisure Activities 27

ENTERTAINMENT
The Wallaces

SPORTS
The hip or shoulder

GAMES
A deck of cards

FOOD AND DRINK
Wine

HEALTH AND FITNESS
Muscles (elbow)

TRAVEL
False. It's equal to approximately two cents.

Answers: Leisure Activities 28

ENTERTAINMENT
Jay Silverheels

SPORTS
The favorite

GAMES
A sports trivia game

FOOD AND DRINK
Insects

HEALTH AND FITNESS
True

TRAVEL
Noon

Leisure Activities 29

ENTERTAINMENT
What is the second novel in the Dune chronicles?

SPORTS
What is the "outrun" in ski jumping?

GAMES
What game features Premium Letter Squares?

FOOD AND DRINK
Introduced in the early 1960s, what was the first of the liquid diet drinks?

HEALTH AND FITNESS
Rubella is the technical name for what disease?

TRAVEL
What body of water washes the western shores of Australia?

Leisure Activities 30

ENTERTAINMENT
Name the Dodie Smith novel that became a popular Walt Disney feature cartoon.

SPORTS
How many feet deep is a football end zone?

GAMES
What shape are most Chinese checker boards?

FOOD AND DRINK
Name the breakfast cereal that has a leprechaun mascot.

HEALTH AND FITNESS
Pertussis vaccine is given to prevent what malady?

TRAVEL
How many time zones does Alaska cover?

ENTERTAINMENT
Dune Messiah

SPORTS
The flat area where skiers slow and stop

GAMES
Scrabble®

FOOD AND DRINK
Metrecal

HEALTH AND FITNESS
German measles

TRAVEL
The Indian Ocean

Answers: Leisure Activities 30

ENTERTAINMENT
One Hundred and One Dalmations

SPORTS
Ten feet

GAMES
Six-pointed stars

FOOD AND DRINK
Lucky Charms

HEALTH AND FITNESS
Whooping cough

TRAVEL
Two

Leisure Activities 31

ENTERTAINMENT
Who won a Tony for his performance as the Leading Player in *Pippin*?

SPORTS
What are the four divisions in the NBA?

GAMES
What is the Milton Bradley board game featuring Bombs, Spies, Flags, and pieces of various military ranks?

FOOD AND DRINK
Austrian Kartoffelbrot is what kind of bread?

HEALTH AND FITNESS
True or false: When providing artificial respiration, the patient's nostrils should usually be pinched shut.

TRAVEL
The flag of which nation is emblazoned with a blue star?

Leisure Activities 32

ENTERTAINMENT
What is the name of Dagwood Bumstead's friend and neighbor?

SPORTS
What was boxer Jack Dempsey's nickname, which was derived from the Colorado town in which he was born?

GAMES
What are the orange Monopoly cards called?

FOOD AND DRINK
What country produces more wine than any other?

HEALTH AND FITNESS
What is the maximum speed at which a human heart can beat in a minute?

TRAVEL
True or false: Australia sprawls across three time zones.

Answers: Leisure Activities 31

ENTERTAINMENT
Ben Vereen

SPORTS
Atlantic, Central, Midwest, and Pacific

GAMES
Stratego

FOOD AND DRINK
Potato bread

HEALTH AND FITNESS
True (unless it's a baby or a small child)

TRAVEL
Israel

Answers: Leisure Activities 32

ENTERTAINMENT
Herb Woodley

SPORTS
The Manassa Mauler

GAMES
Chance

FOOD AND DRINK
Italy

HEALTH AND FITNESS
220 beats per minute

TRAVEL
True

Leisure Activities 33

ENTERTAINMENT
Who wrote *Dracula*?

SPORTS
How does the shotgun differ from most football formations?

GAMES
Name the finance game that features Give and Take Cards.

FOOD AND DRINK
What color is caffeine in its powdered state?

HEALTH AND FITNESS
True or false: People feel hungry when their blood sugar level drops.

TRAVEL
The Red Sea forms the western border of what nation?

Leisure Activities 34

ENTERTAINMENT
Who was the emcee of the original radio and TV versions of *Beat the Clock*?

SPORTS
Who was the first golfer to win the U.S. Open and the U.S. Amateur championships in the same year?

GAMES
Uno is played with   (a) dominoes   (b) cards   (c) dice

FOOD AND DRINK
Name the three varieties of fruit that Post freeze-dried and packaged with corn flakes in the sixties.

HEALTH AND FITNESS
True or false: Fiber decreases the number of calories a person draws from food.

TRAVEL
Bogota is the capital of what South American country?

Answers: Leisure Activities 33

ENTERTAINMENT
Bram Stoker

SPORTS
The quarterback stands a few yards behind the center.

GAMES
Easy Money

FOOD AND DRINK
White

HEALTH AND FITNESS
True

TRAVEL
Saudi Arabia

Answers: Leisure Activities 34

ENTERTAINMENT
Bud Collyer

SPORTS
Charles "Chick" Evans

GAMES
b) cards

FOOD AND DRINK
Strawberries, blueberries, and peaches

HEALTH AND FITNESS
True

TRAVEL
Colombia

Leisure Activities 35

ENTERTAINMENT
On The Mickey Mouse Club's "Circus Day," what two Mouse-keteers were the weightlifters?

SPORTS
In what kind of cartwheel do the hands never touch the ground?

GAMES
Name the videogame in which the player must slow down and permit an ambulance to pass whenever it appears.

FOOD AND DRINK
The name of what food derives from the Latin "lasanum" or "cooking pot"?

HEALTH AND FITNESS
Which one of these should the average adult be able to do for at least thirty seconds? (a) hold his or her breath (b) perform a handstand (c) keep from blinking

TRAVEL
Keflavik is the largest airport in what country?

Leisure Activities 36

ENTERTAINMENT
Name the two Jules Verne novels that feature Captain Nemo.

SPORTS
What are the four divisions of the NHL?

GAMES
What color is Q*Bert? (a) orange (b) green (c) white

FOOD AND DRINK
What cut of beef lies between tenderloin and rump?

HEALTH AND FITNESS
Triskaidekaphobia is a fear of what?

TRAVEL
How many leptas are there in a Greek Drachma?

Answers: Leisure Activities 35

ENTERTAINMENT
Karen and Cubby

SPORTS
Aerial cartwheel

GAMES
Turbo

FOOD AND DRINK
Lasagne

HEALTH AND FITNESS
a) hold their breath

TRAVEL
Iceland

Answers: Leisure Activities 36

ENTERTAINMENT
Twenty Thousand Leagues Under the Sea and *Mysterious Island*

SPORTS
Norris, Adams, Patrick, and Smythe

GAMES
a) orange

FOOD AND DRINK
Sirloin

HEALTH AND FITNESS
The number thirteen

TRAVEL
One hundred

Leisure Activities 37

ENTERTAINMENT
Name the T. S. Eliot opus on which the Broadway musical *Cats* is based.

SPORTS
Name the race established at the Pimlico Race Track, Baltimore, in 1873.

GAMES
Name the game in which players take turns placing discs—black on one side, white on the other—on an eight-by-eight grid.

FOOD AND DRINK
True or false: Shark's tongue is considered the highlight of a Chinese feast.

HEALTH AND FITNESS
R.T. is a medical abbreviation for what kind of technician?

TRAVEL
What is the name of the leading Irish-based airline?

Leisure Activities 38

ENTERTAINMENT
Name the TV comedian who created those musician gorillas, the Nairobi Trio.

SPORTS
In racquetball, what is the call if the serve hits the ground before reaching the front wall?

GAMES
In Monopoly, what separates Indiana Avenue from Kentucky Avenue?

FOOD AND DRINK
What meat is the main ingredient of moussaka?

HEALTH AND FITNESS
What part of the body is cut in a Z-plasty operation?

TRAVEL
How many time zones are there internationally?

ENTERTAINMENT
Old Possum's Book of Practical Cats

SPORTS
The Preakness

GAMES
Othello

FOOD AND DRINK
False. Shark's fin has the honor.

HEALTH AND FITNESS
X-ray Technician

TRAVEL
Aer Lingus

ENTERTAINMENT
Ernie Kovacs

SPORTS
The next player serves

GAMES
A Chance space

FOOD AND DRINK
Lamb

HEALTH AND FITNESS
The skin

TRAVEL
Twenty-four

Leisure Activities 39

ENTERTAINMENT
What was the name of the Jupiter-bound spaceship in *2001: A Space Odyssey*?

SPORTS
True or false: Canonero II won the Triple Crown in 1971.

GAMES
How many dice are used in *Yahtzee*?

FOOD AND DRINK
A food labeled "Florentine" is prepared with what?

HEALTH AND FITNESS
What does a surgeon do with a hemostat?

TRAVEL
Is the air distance greater between New York and Los Angeles, or Paris and New York?

Leisure Activities 40

ENTERTAINMENT
Which one of these is not a Neil Simon play? (a) *Plaza Suite* (b) *California Suite* (c) *The Four Seasons*

SPORTS
What are the NHL's two conferences?

GAMES
What board game from the 1960s, based on a TV show, invited players to, "test your knowledge about top teen entertainers"?

FOOD AND DRINK
True or false: Chianti is a red wine.

HEALTH AND FITNESS
What are the six basic food nutrients?

TRAVEL
Who wrote the best-selling travel tale *Blue Highways*?

ENTERTAINMENT
The *Discovery*

SPORTS
False. The horse won all but the Belmont.

GAMES
Five

FOOD AND DRINK
Spinach

HEALTH AND FITNESS
Clamps a bleeding artery or vein

TRAVEL
Paris and New York (3,638 miles vs. 2,451 miles)

Answers: Leisure Activities 40

ENTERTAINMENT
c) *The Four Seasons*

SPORTS
Prince of Wales and Clarence Campbell

GAMES
Shindig

FOOD AND DRINK
False. It's made with red and white grapes.

HEALTH AND FITNESS
Proteins, fats, vitamins, water, minerals, and carbohydrates

TRAVEL
William Least Heat Moon

Leisure Activities 41

ENTERTAINMENT
"There are certain themes of which the interest is all-absorbing . . ."
begins a Poe tale about taphophobia. Name the story.

SPORTS
Which one of these teams does not belong to the American League
Eastern Division?   (a) Detroit Tigers   (b) Toronto Blue Jays   (c)
New York Mets

GAMES
With what hand is the inmate holding the bars on the Monopoly
jail space?

FOOD AND DRINK
What food and beverage additive, shown in 1969 to cause cancer,
was subsequently withdrawn from the market?

HEALTH AND FITNESS
Which vitamin is needed to maintain visual acuity?

TRAVEL
In what country is Helsinki Airport?

Leisure Activities 42

ENTERTAINMENT
Name the milkman in *Fiddler on the Roof*.

SPORTS
What sport awards the Podoloff Trophy for most valuable player?

GAMES
What is closer to the end in Candyland, peppermint sticks or
lollipops?

FOOD AND DRINK
Name the Ukrainian city that spawned a famous chicken dish.

HEALTH AND FITNESS
Where are the adenoids located?

TRAVEL
What nation's flag is a white cross on a red field?

Answers: Leisure Activities 41

ENTERTAINMENT
"Premature Burial"

SPORTS
c) New York Mets

GAMES
His right

FOOD AND DRINK
Cyclamates

HEALTH AND FITNESS
Vitamin A

TRAVEL
Finland

Answers: Leisure Activities 42

ENTERTAINMENT
Tevye

SPORTS
Basketball

GAMES
Lollipops

FOOD AND DRINK
Kiev

HEALTH AND FITNESS
In the throat (behind the nose)

TRAVEL
Switzerland's

Leisure Activities 43

ENTERTAINMENT
Name the TV series in which Roddy McDowall played the shaggy Galen.

SPORTS
What is a "field goal" in bowling?

GAMES
How many rooms are there in *Clue*?

FOOD AND DRINK
What kind of salad would consist of apples, celery, walnuts, raisins, and mayonnaise?

HEALTH AND FITNESS
Kelp in the diet provides the body with what important element?

TRAVEL
In what country would a traveler spend forints and fillers?

Leisure Activities 44

ENTERTAINMENT
What Hollywood producer-entrepreneur did Alfred Hitchcock envy, commenting, "If he doesn't like an actor, he just tears him up"?

SPORTS
J. Paul Getty was once a sparring partner for what heavyweight champion?

GAMES
How many points are Scrabble players awarded for using all seven letters?

FOOD AND DRINK
What kind of dressing is the result of mixing mayonnaise and catsup?

HEALTH AND FITNESS
How many wisdom teeth does the average adult have?

TRAVEL
What is the capital of Czechoslovakia?

ENTERTAINMENT
Planet of the Apes

SPORTS
When the ball rolls between a split and doesn't strike the pins

GAMES
Nine

FOOD AND DRINK
Waldorf salad

HEALTH AND FITNESS
Iodine

TRAVEL
Hungary

Answers: Leisure Activities 44

ENTERTAINMENT
Walt Disney

SPORTS
Jack Dempsey

GAMES
Fifty

FOOD AND DRINK
Russian dressing

HEALTH AND FITNESS
Four

TRAVEL
Prague

Leisure Activities 45

ENTERTAINMENT
Name the 1971 film starring one member of the movies' *Odd Couple*, and directed by the other.

SPORTS
With what team did football great Red Grange sign after leaving the University of Illinois?

GAMES
Which one of these films did not become an Atari video game? (a) *Raiders of the Lost Ark* (b) *E.T.* (c) *Superman II*

FOOD AND DRINK
Tokaj is the most popular wine produced by what country?

HEALTH AND FITNESS
In a healthy human, which of these usually takes four to six minutes? (a) a mosquito bite to start itching (b) food to reach the stomach (c) coagulation

TRAVEL
True or false: The International Date Line has to take a sudden cut to the west to avoid slashing through part of Alaska.

Leisure Activities 46

ENTERTAINMENT
In 1959, who played the character Milton Armitage on *The Many Loves of Dobie Gillis*?

SPORTS
What sport's hall of fame is located in Canton, Ohio?

GAMES
What does "NN" stand for in the "Baby Boomer" edition of *Trivial Pursuit®*?

FOOD AND DRINK
What kind of food is sweetbread?

HEALTH AND FITNESS
What does bone marrow manufacture?

TRAVEL
Name the country surrounded by Brazil, Argentina, and Bolivia.

Answers: Leisure Activities 45

ENTERTAINMENT
Kotch. Walter Matthau starred, Jack Lemon directed.

SPORTS
The Chicago Bears

GAMES
c) *Superman II*

FOOD AND DRINK
Hungary

HEALTH AND FITNESS
c) coagulation

TRAVEL
True

Answers: Leisure Activities 46

ENTERTAINMENT
Warren Beatty

SPORTS
Football's

GAMES
Nightly News

FOOD AND DRINK
The pancreas of an animal (usually a calf or lamb)

HEALTH AND FITNESS
Blood cells

TRAVEL
Paraguay

Leisure Activities 47

ENTERTAINMENT
What form of stage entertainment derives its name from the French, "Chanson du vau de Vire"—"Song of the vale of Vire"?

SPORTS
What sport uses a ball that cannot weigh more than 1.62 ounces or be smaller than 1.68 inches in diameter?

GAMES
How many pieces does each player have in chess?

FOOD AND DRINK
In Mexico, what is round, flat, unleavened bread made from corn meal called?

HEALTH AND FITNESS
True or false: Teflon is used in blood vessel grafting.

TRAVEL
Kingston is the capital of what West Indies dominion?

Leisure Activities 48

ENTERTAINMENT
Name the TV talk-show host whose sidekick was Regis Philbin.

SPORTS
The Philadelphia Flyers' Dick Schultz is the holder of what dubious hockey honor?

GAMES
What was the first laser-disc video game based on a movie hit?

FOOD AND DRINK
What was the candy of E.T.?

HEALTH AND FITNESS
True or false: Both Nautilus and Universal are brands of exercise equipment.

TRAVEL
What state is both west and south of Oklahoma?

ENTERTAINMENT
Vaudeville

SPORTS
Golf

GAMES
Sixteen

FOOD AND DRINK
A tortilla

HEALTH AND FITNESS
True

TRAVEL
Jamaica

Answers: Leisure Activities 48

ENTERTAINMENT
Joey Bishop

SPORTS
Most penalty time served

GAMES
Firefox

FOOD AND DRINK
Reese's Pieces

HEALTH AND FITNESS
True

TRAVEL
Texas

Leisure Activities 49

ENTERTAINMENT
Which TV show regularly awarded The Flying Fickle Finger of
Fate Award?

SPORTS
Which wears toe weights, a trotter or a pacer?

GAMES
Nyout is a popular, ancient game from what country?

FOOD AND DRINK
What company makes Pop Tarts?

HEALTH AND FITNESS
What part of the body are "side-pulls" designed to tone?

TRAVEL
True or false: English is the principal language of Iceland.

Leisure Activities 50

ENTERTAINMENT
Name the famous singer/entertainer whose parents were Charles
and Rose Borach.

SPORTS
What has the pitcher struck if a "beanball" has been tossed?   (a)
the batter's head   (b) the catcher's head   (c) home plate

GAMES
What color is the twenty-dollar bill in Monopoly?

FOOD AND DRINK
Which one of these is not a Drake's product?   (a) Scooter Pie   (b)
Ring Dings   (c) Yodels

HEALTH AND FITNESS
What does an ailurophobic fear?

TRAVEL
North Front Airport serves what 2½-square-mile British colony?

ENTERTAINMENT
Rowan and Martin's Laugh-In

SPORTS
Trotter

GAMES
Korea (both North and South)

FOOD AND DRINK
Kellogg's

HEALTH AND FITNESS
The waist

TRAVEL
False. Icelandic is.

Answers: Leisure Activities 50

ENTERTAINMENT
Fanny Brice

SPORTS
a) the batter's head

GAMES
Green

FOOD AND DRINK
a) Scotter Pie

HEALTH AND FITNESS
Cats

TRAVEL
Gibraltar

Leisure Activities 51

ENTERTAINMENT
Name the film in which Paul Newman played boxer Rocky Graziano.

SPORTS
Name the player who holds the record for bases-on-balls.

GAMES
What decades are covered in *Time the Game*?

FOOD AND DRINK
Which has more calories, a tablespoon of French dressing or a slice of bacon?

HEALTH AND FITNESS
True or false: Gymnophobia is a fear of athletics.

TRAVEL
What country have you reached if you're in Auckland?

Leisure Activities 52

ENTERTAINMENT
What was cartoonist Alfred Gerald Caplin better known as?

SPORTS
How wide is a basketball court?

GAMES
What magazine's name is attached to the new game of *Sell Out*, "the totally unethical game of making it to the top"?

FOOD AND DRINK
Which one of these is not a brand of Celestial Seasonings tea?   (a) Morning Zinger   (b) Pelican Punch   (c) Sunburst C

HEALTH AND FITNESS
Name the company responsible for the Love Canal chemical dumping.

TRAVEL
Nadi Airport serves what island group of the British Commonwealth?

Answers: Leisure Activities 51

ENTERTAINMENT
Somebody Up There Likes Me

SPORTS
Babe Ruth

GAMES
1920–1980

FOOD AND DRINK
French dressing, by three-to-one

HEALTH AND FITNESS
False. It's a fear of nakedness.

TRAVEL
New Zealand

Answers: Leisure Activities 52

ENTERTAINMENT
Al Capp

SPORTS
Fifty feet

GAMES
National Lampoon

FOOD AND DRINK
a) Morning Zinger

HEALTH AND FITNESS
Hooker Chemical

TRAVEL
Fiji Islands

Leisure Activities 53

ENTERTAINMENT
What was the name of *The Girl from U.N.C.L.E.*?

SPORTS
What was first used by billiard players in 1806 in order to improve ball control?

GAMES
Blind Alley, in which players both build a secret maze and try to guess the layout of their opponent's, is a variation of what seagoing game?

FOOD AND DRINK
True or false: It takes over three pounds of grapes to produce one bottle of champagne.

HEALTH AND FITNESS
True or false: Pasteurization preserves the enzymes in milk.

TRAVEL
Is it North or South Vietnam that is bordered by the Gulf of Tonkin?

Leisure Activities 54

ENTERTAINMENT
In which Disney film was "When You Wish Upon a Star" introduced?

SPORTS
True or false: A bowling alley is forty feet long.

GAMES
What scholar's name is attached to Waddington's Super Quiz game?

FOOD AND DRINK
The flop 1960s diet drink Minivitine was a spinoff of what successful drink mix?

HEALTH AND FITNESS
What was the number of the red dye that was proved to cause cancer?

TRAVEL
What U.S. state is immediately south of Montreal, Canada?

ENTERTAINMENT
April Dancer

SPORTS
Chalk on the cue tip

GAMES
Battleship

FOOD AND DRINK
True

HEALTH AND FITNESS
False. The opposite is true.

TRAVEL
The north

ENTERTAINMENT
Pinocchio

SPORTS
False. It's sixty feet.

GAMES
Isaac Asimov's

FOOD AND DRINK
Ovaltine

HEALTH AND FITNESS
Number forty

TRAVEL
New York

Leisure Activities 55

ENTERTAINMENT
Name the entertainer whose radio show featured a character named
Parkyakarkas.

SPORTS
What was introduced in 1865 to make boxing safer?

GAMES
Which one of these is *not* the subject of a classic board game?   (a)
Uncle Wiggly   (b) Pick Axe Pete   (c) The Shmoe

FOOD AND DRINK
Name the beer introduced in 1961 to take the head off sales of
imported beers.

HEALTH AND FITNESS
What is the hormone that stimulates the development of male
characteristics?

TRAVEL
Which is further north, San Francisco or Washington, D.C.?

Leisure Activities 56

ENTERTAINMENT
Who is Frederic's love in *The Pirates of Penzance*?

SPORTS
In 1946, the NFL's Cleveland franchise moved to what city?

GAMES
Selchow and Righter's RSVP is frequently referred to as a vertical
version of what game?

FOOD AND DRINK
Which one of these was not a 1960s snack food?   (a) Tricksters   (b) Dippy Canoes   (c) Salty Surfers

HEALTH AND FITNESS
Should someone suffering from nosebleed hold his or her head
erect or tilt it back?

TRAVEL
True or false: The Texas cities of El Paso and Dallas are in different
time zones.

ENTERTAINMENT
Eddie Cantor

SPORTS
The Marquis of Queensberry rules

GAMES
b) Pick Axe Pete

FOOD AND DRINK
Michelob

HEALTH AND FITNESS
Testosterone

TRAVEL
Washington, D.C.

ENTERTAINMENT
Mabel

SPORTS
Los Angeles

GAMES
Scrabble®

FOOD AND DRINK
a) Tricksters

HEALTH AND FITNESS
Hold it erect (blood may otherwise trickle down throat)

TRAVEL
True

Leisure Activities 57

ENTERTAINMENT
What is the number of Sherlock Holmes's residence on Baker Street?

SPORTS
What two teams played in the first intercollegiate football game?

GAMES
What do the letters stand for in TSR Games?

FOOD AND DRINK
True or false: Vanilla is used in the manufacture of chocolate.

HEALTH AND FITNESS
A labial nerve provides sensation to what part of the body?

TRAVEL
The flag of Monaco—red on the top half, white on the bottom—is virtually identical to the flag of what East Indies republic?

Leisure Activities 58

ENTERTAINMENT
What is the alter ego of pulp magazine hero Lamont Cranston?

SPORTS
In what city is the Sugar Bowl played?

GAMES
Which one of these Robert Heinlein novels became the basis for a top-selling game?   (a) *Starship Troopers*   (b) *The Number of the Beast*   (c) *The Moon is a Harsh Mistress*

FOOD AND DRINK
True or false: Bordeaux produces only red wine.

HEALTH AND FITNESS
Scurvy is caused by a deficiency of what vitamin?

TRAVEL
In what country would a traveler spend satangs and bahts, a form of currency?

Answers: Leisure Activities 57

ENTERTAINMENT
221-B

SPORTS
Princeton and Rutgers (1869)

GAMES
Tactical Studies Rules

FOOD AND DRINK
True

HEALTH AND FITNESS
The facial lips

TRAVEL
Indonesia

Answers: Leisure Activities 58

ENTERTAINMENT
The Shadow

SPORTS
New Orleans

GAMES
a) *Starship Troopers*

FOOD AND DRINK
False. It produces both red and white.

HEALTH AND FITNESS
Vitamin C

TRAVEL
Thailand

Leisure Activities 59

ENTERTAINMENT
Michael Jackson won a Grammy for a spoken-word album based on what motion picture?

SPORTS
How many dimples are there on a golf ball?

GAMES
Space Armada and Astro Battle are variations of what video-game classic?

FOOD AND DRINK
What film inspired the snack food Screaming Yellow Zonkers?

HEALTH AND FITNESS
True or false: Mumps are not contagious once the glands begin to swell.

TRAVEL
In what world capital is the Forbidden City located?

Leisure Activities 60

ENTERTAINMENT
What is L'il Abner's last name?

SPORTS
What was the first football team to introduce emblems on the helmet?

GAMES
Which one of these was not an arcade video game?   (a) Centipede   (b) Millipede   (c) Octopi

FOOD AND DRINK
True or false: Six ounces of ginger ale has slightly more calories than a tablespoon of peanut butter.

HEALTH AND FITNESS
What is the more commonly used name for riboflavin?

TRAVEL
Name the famous mausoleum located in Agra, India.

Answers: Leisure Activities 59

ENTERTAINMENT
E.T., The Extraterrestrial

SPORTS
336

GAMES
Space Invaders

FOOD AND DRINK
Yellow Submarine

HEALTH AND FITNESS
False. Mumps are contagious as long as the swelling lasts.

TRAVEL
Peking, China

Answers: Leisure Activities 60

ENTERTAINMENT
Yokum

SPORTS
The Los Angeles Rams

GAMES
c) Octopi

FOOD AND DRINK
False. It has fifty percent fewer calories.

HEALTH AND FITNESS
Vitamin B_2

TRAVEL
The Taj Mahal

Leisure Activities 61

ENTERTAINMENT
Calibos, the Kraken, and Medusa were among the adversaries
hero Harry Hamlin faced in what 1981 film?

SPORTS
What color is the caution flag in auto racing?

GAMES
Which is the better hand in poker, two pair or three of a kind?

FOOD AND DRINK
Which one of these is *not* a tropical fruit?   (a) mango   (b) papaya   (c) fig

HEALTH AND FITNESS
Sugars and starches compose what basic food group?

TRAVEL
What American state lies directly beneath Vancouver, British Columbia, Canada?

Leisure Activities 62

ENTERTAINMENT
In what long-running Broadway musical did Jim Dale encourage
people to "join the circus"?

SPORTS
Where is the National Baseball Hall of Fame?

GAMES
In Monopoly, how much less does Park Place cost than Boardwalk?

FOOD AND DRINK
What is the more familiar name of the Queensland nut or bush
nut?

HEALTH AND FITNESS
Name the mineral that plays a large part in determining the strength
of teeth and bones.

TRAVEL
Name the only U.S. state to border four of the five Great Lakes.

Answers: Leisure Activities 61

ENTERTAINMENT
Clash of the Titans

SPORTS
Yellow

GAMES
Three of a kind

FOOD AND DRINK
c) fig

HEALTH AND FITNESS
Carbohydrates

TRAVEL
Washington

Answers: Leisure Activities 62

ENTERTAINMENT
Barnum

SPORTS
Cooperstown, New York

GAMES
Fifty dollars

FOOD AND DRINK
Macadamia nut

HEALTH AND FITNESS
Calcium

TRAVEL
Michigan

Leisure Activities 63

ENTERTAINMENT
Who was Frank Reynolds's Chicago-based co-anchor on The ABC Evening News?

SPORTS
What is it called when a baseball player takes second base because a hit ball bounces over the outfield fence?

GAMES
Which one of these movies did *not* inspire a home video game?   (a) *Fantastic Voyage*   (b) *Alien*   (c) *2001: A Space Odyssey*

FOOD AND DRINK
Within ten calories either way, what is the caloric content of a tablespoon of sugar?

HEALTH AND FITNESS
What mineral makes it possible for the blood to take oxygen from the lungs and bring it to cells?

TRAVEL
Which city is farther west, Atlanta, Georgia, or Columbus, Ohio?

Leisure Activities 64

ENTERTAINMENT
What is the name of Anne Rice's best-selling novel about the undead?

SPORTS
Which one of these teams is not a part of the NBA's Pacific Division?   (a) Utah Jazz   (b) Phoenix Suns   (c) Seattle Super-sonics

GAMES
What was the only rock group to serve as the basis for both a home and arcade video game?

FOOD AND DRINK
What valley is the United States' oldest wine-growing region?

HEALTH AND FITNESS
Vegetables and fruits, dairy products, and protein products are three of the Basic Four staples of a good diet. What is the fourth?

TRAVEL
Name the sea that lies to the north of Iran.

Answers: Leisure Activities 63

ENTERTAINMENT
Max Robinson

SPORTS
Ground-rule double

GAMES
c) *2001: A Space Odyssey*

FOOD AND DRINK
Fifty

HEALTH AND FITNESS
Iron

TRAVEL
Atlanta, Georgia

Answers: Leisure Activities 64

ENTERTAINMENT
Interview with the Vampire

SPORTS
a) Utah Jazz

GAMES
Journey

FOOD AND DRINK
New York State's Hudson Valley

HEALTH AND FITNESS
Cereal products

TRAVEL
The Caspian Sea

Leisure Activities 65

ENTERTAINMENT
What is the comic book alter ego of young Peter Parker?

SPORTS
In bowling, a gutter shot is   (a) a ball that falls in to the gutter   (b) a ball that skirts the gutter then curves toward the pins   (c) a ball that takes down one pin of a 7-10 split

GAMES
The object of what card game is to meld sets of seven or more cards?

FOOD AND DRINK
What kind of food is gazpacho?

HEALTH AND FITNESS
In conversion hysteria, mental anxieties are converted to what?

TRAVEL
What is the only country with a nonrectangular flag?

Leisure Activities 66

ENTERTAINMENT
Name the 1982 Tony Award-winning Broadway play about the life of an Italian film director.

SPORTS
What boxing classification falls between a bantamweight and a lightweight?

GAMES
Name the game that uses a forty-eight card deck.

FOOD AND DRINK
What is the culinary term for a meat that has been browned lightly, stewed, and served in a sauce made of its own stock?

HEALTH AND FITNESS
The islets of Langerhans are located in   (a) the eyes   (b) the pancreas   (c) the lungs

TRAVEL
Is Nazareth in the north or south of Israel?

ENTERTAINMENT
Spider-Man

SPORTS
b) a ball that skirts the gutter then curves toward the pins

GAMES
Canasta

FOOD AND DRINK
Soup

HEALTH AND FITNESS
Physical symptoms

TRAVEL
Nepal. It consists of two triangular pennants, one atop the other.

Answers: Leisure Activities 66

ENTERTAINMENT
Nine

SPORTS
A featherweight

GAMES
Pinochle

FOOD AND DRINK
Fricassee

HEALTH AND FITNESS
b) The pancreas

TRAVEL
North

Leisure Activities 67

ENTERTAINMENT
What was the name of comedian Steve Martin's first album?

SPORTS
What boxer got his nickname from his "sweet" manner of fighting—punching hard while maintaining his cool, neat look?

GAMES
In chess, does the white queen go on the dark or light space?

FOOD AND DRINK
What company produces TV dinners?

HEALTH AND FITNESS
What is an oocyte?

TRAVEL
When a traveler deplanes at Schwechat Airport, what country is he or she in?

Leisure Activities 68

ENTERTAINMENT
What comedy troupe consists of John Cleese, Michael Palin, Eric Idle, Terry Gilliam, Graham Chapman and Terry Jones?

SPORTS
How many points are awarded in a football "safety"?

GAMES
Which three pieces surround a king in chess?

FOOD AND DRINK
What French term means "cooking with art and high style"?

HEALTH AND FITNESS
Is it an optometrist or an optician who examines the eyes to determine whether glasses are needed?

TRAVEL
What is the capital of Portugal?

ENTERTAINMENT
Let's Get Small

SPORTS
"Sugar Ray" Robinson

GAMES
The light

FOOD AND DRINK
Swanson

HEALTH AND FITNESS
An egg cell before it is fertilized

TRAVEL
Austria

Answers: Leisure Activities 68

ENTERTAINMENT
Monty Python

SPORTS
Two

GAMES
The queen, a pawn, and a bishop

FOOD AND DRINK
Haute cuisine

HEALTH AND FITNESS
Optometrist

TRAVEL
Lisbon

Leisure Activities 69

ENTERTAINMENT
Name the 1964–65 sitcom George Burns did *without* Gracie Allen.

SPORTS
What is an "eagle" in golf?

GAMES
Which one of these is a possible murder weapon in the board game, Clue?   (a) a rope   (b) a brick   (c) a garrotte

FOOD AND DRINK
What is the Japanese word for batter-dipped, deep-fried fish or vegetables?

HEALTH AND FITNESS
True or false: Hair yanked out by the roots will not grow back.

TRAVEL
What is the only nation that has a map on its flag?

Leisure Activities 70

ENTERTAINMENT
Which one of these actors did not play Al Capone on film?   (a) Ernest Borgnine   (b) Rod Steiger   (c) Paul Muni

SPORTS
In gymnastics, what is the name for a backward handspring?

GAMES
What is the strongest poker hand?

FOOD AND DRINK
The fiber coir, used for stuffing mattresses, comes from the shell of what food?

HEALTH AND FITNESS
What is the medical term for a person's fear of fear?

TRAVEL
Central America and South America are joined at what two countries, respectively?

ENTERTAINMENT
Wendy and Me

SPORTS
Two strokes under par on any given hole

GAMES
a) a rope

FOOD AND DRINK
Tempura

HEALTH AND FITNESS
False

TRAVEL
Cyprus

Answers: Leisure Activities 70

ENTERTAINMENT
a) Ernest Borgnine

SPORTS
Flic-flac

GAMES
A royal flush

FOOD AND DRINK
The coconut

HEALTH AND FITNESS
Phobophobia

TRAVEL
Panama and Colombia

Leisure Activities 71

ENTERTAINMENT
The action of what recent movie was triggered by the command,
"Let's play thermonuclear war"?

SPORTS
What is the ruling if a catcher interferes with a batter's swing?

GAMES
What is the graphic design on the game board for Risk?

FOOD AND DRINK
What condiment brand name is shown on the packaging inside a
red banner?

HEALTH AND FITNESS
True or false: Daily shampooing is bad for hair.

TRAVEL
What is the capital of South Dakota?

Leisure Activities 72

ENTERTAINMENT
"Well early in the springtime we round up the cattle . . ." is the
opening line of what famous cowboy folk song?

SPORTS
What is the name of the South African Olympic runner who races
barefoot?

GAMES
What popular board game advertised itself as "the fashionable
English game"?

FOOD AND DRINK
Which direction does the pitcher lip face on Kool-Aid packaging?

HEALTH AND FITNESS
"Costal" is a term that refers to what part of the body?

TRAVEL
Name the only state touched by the St. Lawrence River.

ENTERTAINMENT
WarGames

SPORTS
The batter walks

GAMES
A map of the world

FOOD AND DRINK
French's

HEALTH AND FITNESS
False

TRAVEL
Pierre

Answers: Leisure Activities 72

ENTERTAINMENT
Git Along Little Dogies

SPORTS
Zola Budd

GAMES
Sorry!

FOOD AND DRINK
Left

HEALTH AND FITNESS
The ribs

TRAVEL
New York

Leisure Activities 73

ENTERTAINMENT
Who wrote *Cruel Shoes*?

SPORTS
What baseball area, near the dugout, is five feet in diameter?

GAMES
Black Lady—in which the Queen of spades is worth thirteen points—is a popular variation of what card game?

FOOD AND DRINK
What is the difference between British wine and English wine?

HEALTH AND FITNESS
What does D.D.S. stand for in dentistry?

TRAVEL
True or false: The flag of Rwanda has a big, black *R* in the middle.

Leisure Activities 74

ENTERTAINMENT
Whose comic strip adventures were set in Slumberland?

SPORTS
What is the basketball term for a scoring attempt that misses the hoop, net, and backboard?

GAMES
In cards, what is "ruffing power"?

FOOD AND DRINK
What color is the bonnet of the raisin-making Sun Maid?

HEALTH AND FITNESS
What is the substance in red blood cells that carries oxygen from the lungs and, after circulation through the body, returns with carbon dioxide?

TRAVEL
If a traveler sees a yellow flag, what does that mean?

ENTERTAINMENT
Steve Martin

SPORTS
The on-deck circle

GAMES
Hearts

FOOD AND DRINK
British wine is made from imported grapes; English wine is not.

HEALTH AND FITNESS
Doctor of Dental Surgery

TRAVEL
True

Answers: Leisure Activities 74

ENTERTAINMENT
Little Nemo's

SPORTS
An air ball

GAMES
The power to trump

FOOD AND DRINK
Red

HEALTH AND FITNESS
Hemoglobin

TRAVEL
The area is quarantined

Leisure Activities 75

ENTERTAINMENT
What animal character did author Eric Knight create in 1938?

SPORTS
What is the lightest boxing classification?

GAMES
Each player has how many checker pieces on each row at the beginning of play?

FOOD AND DRINK
True or false: The U.S. produces more peaches annually than any other fruit.

HEALTH AND FITNESS
What is the term that describes one who cannot sleep?

TRAVEL
Northern Japan is due east of what country?

Leisure Activities 76

ENTERTAINMENT
Whenever radio's Fibber McGee opened his closet, what instrument came tumbling out?

SPORTS
What is the baseball term for a home run that brings in four runs?

GAMES
What game derives its name from the Persian (Iranian) word "shah"?

FOOD AND DRINK
On a menu, the term flambé indicates what?

HEALTH AND FITNESS
What does an otoscope permit doctors to examine?

TRAVEL
Which one of these ports is *not* on the English Channel? (a) Liverpool (b) Brighton (c) Portsmouth

Answers: Leisure Activities 75

ENTERTAINMENT
Lassie

SPORTS
Light Flyweight

GAMES
Four

FOOD AND DRINK
False. Apples beat peaches nearly four to one.

HEALTH AND FITNESS
Insomniac

TRAVEL
The USSR

Answers: Leisure Activities 76

ENTERTAINMENT
A mandolin

SPORTS
A grand slam

GAMES
Chess ("shah" means "king")

FOOD AND DRINK
Flambé indicates that the food is served flaming.

HEALTH AND FITNESS
The interior of the ear

TRAVEL
a) Liverpool

Leisure Activities 77

ENTERTAINMENT
Who was the owner of the circus in *Circus Boy*?

SPORTS
What baseball teams played in the first major league night game?

GAMES
How many pieces does each backgammon player receive?

FOOD AND DRINK
Which has a softer head, iceberg or butterhead lettuce?

HEALTH AND FITNESS
Night blindness can result from a lack of what vitamin?

TRAVEL
Santiago is the capital of what country?

Leisure Activities 78

ENTERTAINMENT
On TV's *Arrest and Trial*, Detective Sergeant Nick Anderson handled arrests and John Egan, Esquire, handled trials. Who played these characters?

SPORTS
Who was baseball's "Say Hey" kid?

GAMES
"The Game of Political Power" is the subtitle for what popular board game?

FOOD AND DRINK
What is the principal ingredient of sauerkraut?

HEALTH AND FITNESS
Which vitamin is ascorbic acid?

TRAVEL
Which is farther from London, Rome or Chicago?

ENTERTAINMENT
Big Tim Champion

SPORTS
Philadelphia and Cincinnati

GAMES
Fifteen

FOOD AND DRINK
Butterhead

HEALTH AND FITNESS
Vitamin A

TRAVEL
Chile

Answers: Leisure Activities 78

ENTERTAINMENT
Ben Gazarra and Chuck Connors, respectively

SPORTS
Willie Mays

GAMES
Lie, Cheat & Steal

FOOD AND DRINK
Cabbage

HEALTH AND FITNESS
Vitamin C

TRAVEL
Chicago (3,960 vs. 892 air miles)

Leisure Activities 79

ENTERTAINMENT
Who did Chester Morris play in fourteen motion pictures?

SPORTS
What is the name of basketball's San Antonio franchise?

GAMES
Which Parker Brothers game features upright dollar signs as playing pieces?

FOOD AND DRINK
In Japan, what dish of meat, soy sauce, bean curd, and greens is known as the "friendship dish"?

HEALTH AND FITNESS
Rickets can be caused in youngsters by a lack of what vitamin?

TRAVEL
True or false: There is an Upper Volta in Africa, but no Lower Volta.

Leisure Activities 80

ENTERTAINMENT
Anthony Daniels provided the voice for (a) C-3PO in *Star Wars* (b) Hal in *2001: A Space Odyssey* (c) Mr. Ed on TV

SPORTS
What is the name of the diving position in which the knees are drawn against the chest?

GAMES
Name the game with a picture of Vincent Price on the box.

FOOD AND DRINK
What is the principal ingredient of a Margarita?

HEALTH AND FITNESS
True or false: Ultraviolet light accelerates hair growth.

TRAVEL
What nation is closest to the easternmost part of the Soviet Union?

Answers: Leisure Activities 79

ENTERTAINMENT
Boston Blackie

SPORTS
The Spurs

GAMES
Billionaire

FOOD AND DRINK
Sukiyaki

HEALTH AND FITNESS
Vitamin D

TRAVEL
True

Answers: Leisure Activities 80

ENTERTAINMENT
a) c-3PO in *Star Wars*

SPORTS
A tuck

GAMES
Hangman

FOOD AND DRINK
Tequila

HEALTH AND FITNESS
False

TRAVEL
The U.S. (at Alaska)

Leisure Activities 81

ENTERTAINMENT
What is the name of Robert Redford's team in *The Natural*?
SPORTS
What was the score of the Superbowl the year the New York Jets beat the Baltimore Colts?
GAMES
What are the dots called on a domino?
FOOD AND DRINK
True or false: Tomatoes are vegetables.
HEALTH AND FITNESS
Desenex powder is used to treat what affliction?
TRAVEL
Which reaches farther south, the tip of Florida or the tip of Texas?

Leisure Activities 82

ENTERTAINMENT
Name the musical that features "The Impossible Dream."
SPORTS
Which one of these is *not* a team in the National Football Conference's Western Division? (a) Atlanta Falcons (b) New Orleans Saints (c) San Diego Chargers
GAMES
Name the Parker Brothers game in which great art—as well as forgeries—are bought and sold.
FOOD AND DRINK
Name the spirit added to milk, beaten eggs, and sugar to make a Tom and Jerry.
HEALTH AND FITNESS
Which is less accurate, an oral or rectal thermometer?
TRAVEL
Which is the northernmost of the Great Lakes?

Answers: Leisure Activities 81

ENTERTAINMENT
The New York Knights

SPORTS
16–7

GAMES
Pips

FOOD AND DRINK
False. The tomato is a fruit.

HEALTH AND FITNESS
Athlete's foot

TRAVEL
Florida

Answers: Leisure Activities 82

ENTERTAINMENT
Man of La Mancha

SPORTS
c) San Diego Chargers

GAMES
Masterpiece

FOOD AND DRINK
Rum

HEALTH AND FITNESS
Oral (by approximately .5 degrees)

TRAVEL
Lake Superior

Leisure Activities 83

ENTERTAINMENT
What famous comic strip, subtitled, "A Saga of the West," was about an army sergeant stationed in California?

SPORTS
In 1920, what hockey team set the all-time record of the most goals (16) in a single game?

GAMES
What classic Milton Bradley game has plastic hills, buildings, and a large spinner built right into the board?

FOOD AND DRINK
The fabled land of Cockaigne fed its natives small, stiff cakes. What are these cakes called?

HEALTH AND FITNESS
What kind of vaccine is administered in 14 to 21 daily injections, followed by boosters 10 to 20 days later?

TRAVEL
The Japanese yen is made up of one hundred of what smaller currency.

Leisure Activities 84

ENTERTAINMENT
What radio show opened with the words, "Lights out—*everybody*!"?

SPORTS
Only one Triple Crown winner ever sired a Triple Crown winner. Name both horses.

GAMES
What war is the setting for Milton Bradley's classic Battle Cry?

FOOD AND DRINK
Pilaf is what cooked in a broth of meat or poultry?

HEALTH AND FITNESS
Because of experiments performed with the rhesus monkey, what blood condition was named in the monkey's honor?

TRAVEL
Pearl Harbor is on what Hawaiian island?

ENTERTAINMENT
Casey Ruggles

SPORTS
The Montreal Canadiens

GAMES
The Game of Life

FOOD AND DRINK
Cookies

HEALTH AND FITNESS
Rabies

TRAVEL
Sen

Answers: Leisure Activities 84

ENTERTAINMENT
Lights Out

SPORTS
Gallant Fox was the father, Omaha the offspring

GAMES
The Civil War

FOOD AND DRINK
Rice

HEALTH AND FITNESS
Rh factor

TRAVEL
Oahu

Leisure Activities 85

ENTERTAINMENT
Which one of these novels was not written by Eric van Lustbader?—(a) *Sirens* (b) *Black Heart* (c) *Sphinx*

SPORTS
What number did Ty Cobb wear?

GAMES
Name the English counterparts for *pique, coeur, carreau,* and *trefle*.

FOOD AND DRINK
Welsh rarebit is melted cheese, milk, and usually beer or ale served over what?

HEALTH AND FITNESS
An electroencephalogram is a graphic picture of activity in what organ?

TRAVEL
Where is Capitoline Hill?

Leisure Activities 86

ENTERTAINMENT
Radio's Stella Dallas used the nickname "Lolly Baby" for (a) her daughter (b) her dog (c) her husband

SPORTS
What is the term used to describe the shadowboxing aspect of karate?

GAMES
Whist is an early form of what card game?

FOOD AND DRINK
Name the dish that derives from the old French word *alemelle*, literally meaning "thin plate."

HEALTH AND FITNESS
What elastic cartilage closes off the windpipe during swallowing?

TRAVEL
Masada is on the eastern shore of what body of water?

Answers: Leisure Activities 85

ENTERTAINMENT
c) *Sphinx*. It was written by Robin Cook.

SPORTS
None. Numbers weren't initiated until after he'd retired.

GAMES
Diamonds, hearts, clubs, and spades.

FOOD AND DRINK
Toast

HEALTH AND FITNESS
The brain

TRAVEL
Rome

Answers: Leisure Activities 86

ENTERTAINMENT
a) her daughter

SPORTS
Kata

GAMES
Bridge

FOOD AND DRINK
Omelet

HEALTH AND FITNESS
The epiglottis

TRAVEL
The Dead Sea

Leisure Activities 87

ENTERTAINMENT
On which album cover did John Lennon and his wife Yoko Ono appear nude?

SPORTS
In baseball terminology, what is the "meat hand"?

GAMES
In Gin Rummy, is the ace the same value as a face card?

FOOD AND DRINK
Adding what to a mere martini will make it a Gibson?

HEALTH AND FITNESS
What is impaired by dyslexia?

TRAVEL
True or false: Loch Ness is a famous Irish lake.

Leisure Activities 88

ENTERTAINMENT
Name the film legend who starred in the CBS series *Hawkins*.

SPORTS
In what sports is a cesta used to propel a ball around a fronton?

GAMES
Name the Invicta game in which one player constructs a code of four pegs, an arrangement his or her opponent tries to deduce by trial, error, and logic.

FOOD AND DRINK
What is the name for an oblong cream puff that has been filled and topped with icing?

HEALTH AND FITNESS
What is the name given to the organic catalysts of various processes, actions, and interactions in the body?

TRAVEL
What state is bordered by both Carolinas?

Answers: Leisure Activities 87

ENTERTAINMENT
Two Virgins

SPORTS
The hand without a glove

GAMES
No. It's value is one.

FOOD AND DRINK
An onion

HEALTH AND FITNESS
The ability to read

TRAVEL
False. It's in Scotland.

Answers: Leisure Activities 88

ENTERTAINMENT
James Stewart

SPORTS
Jai alai

GAMES
Master Mind

FOOD AND DRINK
An eclair

HEALTH AND FITNESS
Enzymes

TRAVEL
Georgia

Leisure Activities 89

ENTERTAINMENT
What is the name of the town invaded in Steven Spielberg's 1984 film, *Gremlins*?

SPORTS
In boxing, what's the name for an illegal punch to the small of the back?

GAMES
When originally released, what was the unlikely name of the Parker Brothers game *All the King's Men*?

FOOD AND DRINK
What salty snack food gets its name from the Medieval Latin *bracellus* or "bracelet"?

HEALTH AND FITNESS
Blennophobia describes a fear of (a) religious objects (b) slime (c) blushing

TRAVEL
What two states are home to Death Valley?

Leisure Activities 90

ENTERTAINMENT
What 1960 film made stars of George Hamilton, Jim Hutton, Yvette Mimieux, and Connie Francis?

SPORTS
How many stumps are there on a cricket wicket?

GAMES
How many pawns are there on a chessboard?

FOOD AND DRINK
Name the founder of Weight Watchers.

HEALTH AND FITNESS
Which one of these is not a stimulant? (a) Dexedrine (b) Benzedrine (c) Thorazine

TRAVEL
The busy Ginza district, famous for food and smart shopping, is located in what city?

ENTERTAINMENT
Kingston Falls

SPORTS
A kidney punch

GAMES
Smess: The Ninny's Chess

FOOD AND DRINK
The pretzel

HEALTH AND FITNESS
b) slime

TRAVEL
California and Nevada

Answers: Leisure Activities 90

ENTERTAINMENT
Where the Boys Are

SPORTS
Three

GAMES
Sixteen, eight for each player.

FOOD AND DRINK
Jean Nidetch

HEALTH AND FITNESS
c) Thorazine

TRAVEL
Tokyo

Leisure Activities 91

ENTERTAINMENT
What rubbery substance did Fred MacMurray invent in *The Absent Minded Professor*?

SPORTS
Chuck Wepner fell in March, 1975, Ron Lyle in May, and Joe Bugner in July. Who were they boxing?   (a) Muhammad Ali (b) Larry Holmes   (c) Joe Frazier

GAMES
What words are printed above the name of the property on each Monopoly deed?

FOOD AND DRINK
Yellowfin, bluefin, skipjack, and albacore describe what kind of food fish?

HEALTH AND FITNESS
Cerumen is a fancy name for what bodily accumulation?

TRAVEL
What city is home to the Prado, one of the world's greatest art museums?

Leisure Activities 92

ENTERTAINMENT
Who did Bridget love in the prime-time series?

SPORTS
What is the Western equivalent of the Oriental discipline "kendo"?

GAMES
True or false: The King in chess can never be moved more than one space per turn.

FOOD AND DRINK
What kind of dish is the Swedish artsoppa, made with peas and ham?

HEALTH AND FITNESS
True or false: Enamel-eating bacteria are responsible for tooth decay.

TRAVEL
In what country would a traveler find words spelled with the letters "resh," "kuf," and "tet"?

Answers: Leisure Activities 91

ENTERTAINMENT
Flubber

SPORTS
a) Muhammed Ali

GAMES
"Title Deed"

FOOD AND DRINK
Tuna

HEALTH AND FITNESS
Earwax

TRAVEL
Madrid

Answers: Leisure Activities 92

ENTERTAINMENT
Bernie

SPORTS
Fencing

GAMES
False. It moves two when castled.

FOOD AND DRINK
Soup

HEALTH AND FITNESS
False. The cause is acid produced by bacteria acting on food.

TRAVEL
Israel

Leisure Activities 93

ENTERTAINMENT
Name the broadway musical about carnival barker Billy Bigelow.

SPORTS
How many bases does a player get after hitting a "bleeder"?

GAMES
What magazine sponsored a board game in which the object was to lose all your money?

FOOD AND DRINK
What is the name for an Italian dish consisting of olives, anchovies, salami, celery, and other appetizers?

HEALTH AND FITNESS
An electrocardiograph records electrical current produced by what organ?

TRAVEL
On what continent is the Cape of Good Hope located?

Leisure Activities 94

ENTERTAINMENT
Early in the century, "Heigh ho, everybody" was the salutation of what entertainer?

SPORTS
How many players are are there on a cricket team?

GAMES
How many "Energy Dots" are there on a Pac-Man screen?

FOOD AND DRINK
What do Germans call a pot roast of beef marinated in vinegar, sugar, and various seasonings?

HEALTH AND FITNESS
What are the first adult teeth to appear?

TRAVEL
Wishing to visit the largest wine-producing country in South America, where would a traveler go?

Answers: Leisure Activities 93

ENTERTAINMENT
Carousel

SPORTS
One. It's a slow, out-of-the-way grounder.

GAMES
Mad magazine

FOOD AND DRINK
Antipasto

HEALTH AND FITNESS
The heart

TRAVEL
Africa

Answers: Leisure Activities 94

ENTERTAINMENT
Rudy Vallee

SPORTS
Eleven

GAMES
Four

FOOD AND DRINK
Sauerbraten

HEALTH AND FITNESS
The incisors (middle, then lateral)

TRAVEL
Argentina

Leisure Activities 95

ENTERTAINMENT
Who wrote and drew the Steve Canyon comic strip?

SPORTS
What is the championship match sponsored by the *Federation Internationale de Football*?

GAMES
What does "NNM" stand for in the All-Star Sports edition of Trivial Pursuit?

FOOD AND DRINK
What is the name for a Polish cake filled with candied fruits and nuts?

HEALTH AND FITNESS
Lifting exercises using the legs strengthens what large muscle in the front of the thigh?

TRAVEL
What is significant about the Orthlieb Pool in Casablanca, Morocco?

Leisure Activities 96

ENTERTAINMENT
Who played Maid Marian to Sean Connery's Robin Hood in the movie *Robin and Marian*?

SPORTS
Which has the longer handle, a racquet for squash or racquetball?

GAMES
Name the Parker Brothers game played on a grid with yellow and green markers.

FOOD AND DRINK
What meat is usually used to make scaloppine?

HEALTH AND FITNESS
What is irreparably destroyed when the body goes through proteolysis?

TRAVEL
What is the world's third largest ocean?

Answers: Leisure Activities 95

ENTERTAINMENT
Milt Caniff

SPORTS
The World Cup

GAMES
Nicknames

FOOD AND DRINK
Babka

HEALTH AND FITNESS
Quadriceps

TRAVEL
It is the world's largest pool.

Answers: Leisure Activities 96

ENTERTAINMENT
Audrey Hepburn

SPORTS
A squash racquet

GAMES
Pente

FOOD AND DRINK
Veal

HEALTH AND FITNESS
Proteins

TRAVEL
The Indian Ocean

Leisure Activities 97

ENTERTAINMENT
What color is the blood of *Star Trek*'s Mr. Spock?

SPORTS
What term describes the act of a hockey player who fires the puck across an opponent's goal line from behind his or her own red line?

GAMES
A player left holding an odd queen is the loser in what game?

FOOD AND DRINK
Marsala is   (a) a sweet wine   (b) a Spanish pomegranate   (c) a lamb dish

HEALTH AND FITNESS
What is a provitamin?

TRAVEL
What two oceans wash against the shores of the Soviet Union?

Leisure Activities 98

ENTERTAINMENT
In 1953, Otto Preminger's *The Moon is Blue* whipped up a controversy because of the use of what word?

SPORTS
What legendary Chicago Bears coach wore the nickname "Papa Bear"?

GAMES
What is the name of the board-game version of "Capture The Flag"?

FOOD AND DRINK
Tarragon is   (a) a dark wine   (b) an herb seasoning   (c) a Japanese fish dish

HEALTH AND FITNESS
What is the street name for the stimulant Methedrine?

TRAVEL
In what country do shoppers patronize the large department stores GUM and ISUM?

Answers: Leisure Activities 97

ENTERTAINMENT
Green

SPORTS
Icing

GAMES
Old Maid

FOOD AND DRINK
a) a sweet wine

HEALTH AND FITNESS
A substance the body can transform into a vitamin

TRAVEL
The Pacific and the Arctic

Answers: Leisure Activities 98

ENTERTAINMENT
"Virgin"

SPORTS
George Halas

GAMES
Stratego

FOOD AND DRINK
b) an herb seasoning

HEALTH AND FITNESS
Speed

TRAVEL
Russia

Leisure Activities 99

ENTERTAINMENT
Emmett Kelly was the name of the *man*; what was the name of his legendary hobo?

SPORTS
What basketball term describes a shot made at the peak of a jump, from under the basket, with the ball usually bouncing off the backboard?

GAMES
What is the highest a player can score on a single ball in Skee-Ball?

FOOD AND DRINK
What is the "national spice" of Hungary?

HEALTH AND FITNESS
True or false: The eardrum separates the middle ear from the inner ear.

TRAVEL
Which of these is not one of the Balkan States? (a) Albania (b) Bulgaria (c) Austria

---

Leisure Activities 100

ENTERTAINMENT
The Jimi Hendrix Experience premiered at what 1967 rock bash?

SPORTS
True or false: Both the men's and the women's Wimbledon Tennis finals are determined by the best out of five set matches.

GAMES
What determines the result of battles in Risk?

FOOD AND DRINK
Who manufactures Twinkies?

HEALTH AND FITNESS
Are the triceps on the front or the back of the upper arm?

TRAVEL
In the harbor of what Spanish city is there a replica of Columbus's ship?

Answers: Leisure Activities 99

ENTERTAINMENT
Weary Willie

SPORTS
A lay-up

GAMES
Fifty points

FOOD AND DRINK
Paprika

HEALTH AND FITNESS
False. It divides the outer and middle ear.

TRAVEL
c) Austria

Answers: Leisure Activities 100

ENTERTAINMENT
Monterey Pop Festival

SPORTS
False. Men play best of five sets; women play best of three.

GAMES
Rolls of the dice

FOOD AND DRINK
Hostess

HEALTH AND FITNESS
The back

TRAVEL
Barcelona